Mailander House

Restoring a Home Left for Dead

David Morrow

Copyright © 2019 David Morrow

All rights reserved.

Published by Quiscat LLC

Waco, Texas

First printing, February, 2019

All rights reserved.

Printed by IngramSpark

ISBN 978-1-7337536-0-9

Printed in the United States of America

Acknowledgements

Many people have helped with this book. Chip and Joanna Gaines gave us the mojo to find funding and then restore a beautiful old home, and their work crews did a great job with the resources available. Several people read early drafts and offered valuable suggestions including Gail Prescott, Ashley Prescott Lesser, and Alyssa Henry, who read an early draft and found me a great editor, Amy Flint. Amy was instrumental in rearranging the book to enhance coherence, eliminating unnecessary material, and moving it to publication. Susan Drinkard demonstrated an amazing eye for minutiae while proofreading, and Don MacNair performed some magic editing photos and preparing the manuscript for publication. All praise and thanks to Paxton Dove for the amazing cover photo.

Ellen Kast, who is eminently practical, reminded me to follow the KISS principle: Keep It Simple, Stupid. My neighbor, friend, and author of numerous books, Ray Lamb, gave excellent advice about publishing and the business side of book writing. Finally, and most importantly, I want to thank my loving wife, Marla Hendricks DVM, for her unflagging support of this project. Writing a book was much more difficult than I thought it would be, and she stood by me and encouraged me all the way.

"All great literature is one of two stories;
a man goes on a journey,
or a stranger comes to town."

Leo Tolstoy

Table of Contents

Acknowledgements 3

Prologue 7

Part I   How It All Began 11
    Chapter 1   Dave & Marla 11
    Chapter 2   The Search 19
    Chapter 3   The Neighborhood 25

Part II   Fixer-Upper Unleashed 30
    Chapter 4   What It Takes to Be a Fixer Upper 30
    Chapter 5   The Loan Fish 37
    Chapter 6   Hijacked by a Film Crew 41
    Chapter 7   The Reveal 46
    Chapter 8   Bicycle House 51

Part III   Living in a Fixer Upper 59
    Chapter 9   Settling In 59
    Chapter 10   Plumbing Hell 64
    Chapter 11   The Wise Man Built His House Upon the Rock ... 71

Part IV   Mailander House Bed & Breakfast 77
    Chapter 12   Making the Transition 77
    Chapter 13   Strategies for Success 83
    Chapter 14   The Bureaucratic Process 85
    Chapter 15   Unusual Guests 88
    Chapter 16   Reviews 106

Part V   Dave's Previous Experiences 111
    Chapter 17   Youthful Challenges 111
    Chapter 18   Family Ranch 114
    Chapter 19   Behind the Redwood Curtain 116
    Chapter 20   Dad's Fresno House 120

PART VI   Dave & Marla's History 130
    Chapter 21   Dave's Early Years 130
    Chapter 22   Marla's Early Years 136

Epilogue 141

Appendix 1: Waco History 148
   Early History 148
   The Civil War and Reconstruction 149
   World War I Era 151
   World War II Era 152
   The Branch Davidians 154

Appendix 2: Mailander Family History 156

Appendix 3: Bicycle History 158

References 160

About the Author 161

Prologue

My wife, Marla Hendricks, and I were lucky enough to have our house in Waco, Texas remodeled by Magnolia Homes, headed by Chip and Joanna Gaines. So many people have asked about our experience that I decided to share it. Our home was originally built in 1910 by Charles and Fred Mailander, father and son German craftsmen. When we bought the house over one hundred years later, we named it 'Mailander House' to honor their fine design and craftsmanship. The remodel of this house was completed by Magnolia Homes and documented on the *Fixer Upper* TV show in 2014. After its original showing in the first season, our episode has been seen on cable television by over 40 million people. This event has changed our lives dramatically and permanently in a good way.

We think of ourselves as "regular folks" who wound up on a wildly popular TV show hosted by one of America's favorite couples. My wife Marla and her sister Gail were the "characters" primarily filmed on the TV segment. I came in at the end for the reveal of our remodeled home. I say that we are "regular folks;" however, we enjoy older homes with character. The oldest home I have owned was built in 1876. Others I've owned were built in the 1940s. I remodeled a house on my parents' ranch that was at least 100 years old. Marla owns a stone house, called Hound Haven, which was built about 1930. We have done a lot of work on our older homes, and I have done commercial construction work, too. So perhaps we are "regular" but also "different" in our tastes, outlook, and experience.

I could not have written this book alone. My wife, Marla, was the one who initiated contact with Chip and Joanna Gaines and plugged us into the Magnolia remodel energy. I have prepared most of this book at a keyboard. However, getting Marla to sit down and write was like pulling teeth (no one wants to see a grown man grovel and beg). Therefore, I bought a small digital recorder and asked her to tell her stories. They are sprinkled throughout this book (her words appear in italics).

Marla says,

This is Dave Morrow's effort to document a very unusual episode in our lives, which was resurrecting an old house that had been left-for-dead. I am his wife, Marla Hendricks, and I have agreed to be part of this book. The most interesting thing I noticed about reading the first two chapters of <u>Capital Gaines</u> *[Chip Gaines' bestseller] was that I felt I had a lot in common with Chip. He talked about the crazy things he had done and how he always looked on the up-side. He was just relentlessly optimistic about the chances of what he was doing working out okay. I also felt a deep connection to Joanna, the voice of reason, especially when the question was numbers. I think I was gifted with an ability to manage numbers in my mind. I can write them down or I can just add it all up and multiply and do percentages, and I can get very close to the bottom line. My bookkeeper and office manager, Dotti Bolen, no longer bothers to question me when I say how much something is going to cost. She doesn't ask me where the numbers come from. It's just one of those things I know.*

My husband, Dave, does not agree. When I pull numbers out of the air, it gets on his last nerve. Tonight, at supper, he and I were talking about 15-year mortgage rates. That got me thinking, and I wanted to share one of the most interesting parts of my <u>Fixer Upper</u> *experience. When I found the house and asked Chip to come over to see it, he bounced up the steps and said, 'We can do this [buy the house and remodel] for $90,000 tops, and we can just talk to Joanna about it.' Joanna sat down with pencil and paper and said, 'It's going to be $100,000 minimum. I don't know why Chip says those things.' That was where I really began to understand that Joanna's number skills are essential. She uses pencil and paper and is meticulous. I think I am a cross between Joanna and Chip. It's all in the air, and I know I can do it. Joanna uses a tablet and a pencil, and trust me, that's where numbers work, so when I got the final quote, it was right around $100,000, just as Joanna had calculated.*

Now Dave and I are four years down the road, and we are about to have something we can truly put a star by and call capital gains. We have increased the value of an old home by a small amount of money - it's not that much. But we bought right and worked hard to make our house a real beauty.

It may be useful for some readers to learn a bit about Waco. Those who grew up here and know all this can skip ahead to Chapter 1. Further historical details about Waco appear in Appendix 1.

Waco is in the southernmost 15% of the US 48 states, and as such has long, hot summers and mild winters. Annual rainfall amounts vary widely. In some years, it will rain more in one month than in the average year (35 inches); in other years, there have been five-month stretches with no rain at all. To put it mildly, the native animals and plants that live here are tough, and so are many of the people.

Waco is situated at the confluence of two major rivers, the Bosque and Brazos. The Bosque is over 300 miles long and originates in the high, dry plains of the Llano Estacado of west Texas. The Brazos originates in the mountains of New Mexico, and its main section is about 840 miles long, terminating in the Gulf of Mexico near Houston. Periodically over the first 100 years of Waco's history, large floods sometimes wiped out swaths of the town's commercial area. In recent decades, several flood control dams upstream have protected downtown Waco from severe flooding.

Waco also straddles the Balcones Escarpment, the limestone remnant of a former mountain range. This escarpment demarcates two dormant faults and roughly separates east and west Texas; parts of Interstate 35 also follows this line. Waco and the surrounding area are astride a fertile soil deposit, called the Blackland Prairie, that supports a rich assortment of grasses and native trees. The Blackland Prairie generally runs from Fort Worth south to Austin. The area Waco occupies is generally flat to gently rolling with only a few hundred feet of elevation change. However, the two rivers have, over the centuries, carved out bluffs as high as 200 feet from the escarpment.

On May 11, 1953, an F5 tornado (the most powerful level) hit downtown Waco without warning. Entire blocks of large brick buildings were destroyed, 114 people perished, and about 600 were badly injured. This was a devastating blow for downtown as many of the important buildings that were destroyed were not rebuilt but converted to parking lots. The sites of many downtown buildings sit empty even today. After the big tornado, Waco's growth was static for many decades, but that is changing, with much of the new growth powered by the popularity of Magnolia Market and the *Fixer Upper* TV show.

Part I How It All Began

Chapter 1 Dave & Marla

I was blessed to meet my future bride (and remodeling partner), Marla Hendricks DVM, at a very auspicious place: Yosemite National Park, in the heart of the Sierra Nevada Mountains. Marla is the most amazing woman I have ever known. I owe my good luck to my brother-in-law, Evan, who met Marla while they were both on a training run in Fresno. Fresno lies about 70 miles west of Yosemite and is convenient for outdoorsy folks heading up the nearby mountains. Marla and Evan run at about the same pace and liked marathons, so they hit it off quickly.

In 2011, Marla was splitting her time between her Waco clinic and Fresno, where she worked with a master doctor to become board certified as an emergency room veterinarian. Marla has owned a clinic in Waco for several decades but was working under another doctor at a large emergency clinic in Fresno to accrue her required practical training hours.

At the Fresno emergency clinic where her training was conducted, she generally worked all night and went out for a run in the morning before she caught a few hours of sleep. Not a schedule for the faint of heart. Marla was training for her second attempt at the Western States 100, an event that involved 30 hours of continuous trail running. When I discovered this, I began to understand that working all night, or running all night, were 'normal' things for her.

The day we met in Yosemite was chilly but sunny, and Evan, Marla, and I had a great time Nordic skiing on Glacier Point Road. Marla was an accomplished alpine skier; however, the technique for Nordic is different, and there are no lifts for the uphill. Marla was just learning the technique, so we only skied six or seven miles that day. Marla and I hit it off right away, and I fondly remember sharing pizza and hot chocolate at the ski lodge after our day on the trails. As I gazed into her gray-blue eyes, I felt enraptured by her soft Arkansas voice – she was a charming conversationalist and, in her element, so full of joy. I didn't think I stood a chance!

The next time I saw Marla, we skied out to the Ostrander Hut, an old stone building at about 8,500 feet deep in the heart of the Sierra Nevada mountains. Because we had a late start from Yosemite Ski and Snowboard Area (formerly Badger Pass), we arrived at the hut well after dark. I had been there before, and we both had good headlamps, so I was not too worried about finding the hut. For the final few hours of skiing that night, we followed the reflections of small pieces of old license plates nailed high in the trees. As we got close, the hut guardian was out on the trail to meet us. While there was no moon, the sky was clear and brilliant starlight reflected off the snow to help us find our way.

Because we were on a short break from work, we did not ski the peaks above the hut the next day, but after a leisurely breakfast started back to the car at Badger Pass. The snow conditions were difficult coming down the ridge from the hut. Despite the conditions (or perhaps because of them), Marla was having a ball on a new adventure. At lunch, I was ahead and stopped on the trail, removing my skis and setting them in the track upside down to sit on. Marla then arrived and gaily removed her brand-new skis as well.

As she set her skis down, one slid a bit down the track and stopped. I breathed a sigh of relief, as we were ensconced on the side of a large ridge – probably 800 feet high, and steep. Marla thought it was funny how the first ski slid down the track and settled in, so she gave her second ski a nudge to join the first. At that moment I just about died thinking, "That is a terrible idea" – and sure enough, the second ski took off down the steep embankment into the forest below. I watched that ski go for as long as I could, but it was moving quickly, and I lost sight of it somewhere down in the trees. I started to have doubts about the reliability of my companion and wondered if this potentially budding romance was going to work out in the long-term.

We had about eight miles left to get back to the car, and it was going to be very slow for her on one ski. So, we undertook the arduous task of hiking down that steep snow-clad slope to find her ski. I kept telling myself, Dave, keep your big mouth shut and smile. After several hours of punching through crusty snow, we gave up without finding her ski. As the day grew to a close, the snow was getting icy after melting in the sun during the afternoon. Marla tried to get out with one ski, but we eventually wound up walking for miles. We arrived at the car well after dark. She thought this was all magical fun and laughed and giggled the whole time. Me, not so much.

While I did have questions about Marla's mountaineering judgment and awareness of hazards, she and I kept skiing together. When spring arrived, we started hiking in the foothills, working our way up into the higher mountains as summer came. And with the spring wildflowers, our romance grew from a crush to real love. I could not spend enough time with her, and I was lonely when she had to go back to Waco every few weeks. When she was in California, all we could do was plan our next adventure.

After a few shorter hikes of three or four days, that autumn we took a ten-day backpacking trip into a remote part of northern Yosemite National Park that few people ever visit. The magic of silent sunrises and gorgeous sunsets was unsurpassed, and we experienced profound solitude and privacy. Yosemite has four million visitors annually – but they mostly stay in the Valley; we had found our place of silence amid some of the most beautiful mountains in the world.

Some might call us crazy, but immediately after that 10-day backpacking trip in the Sierras, we left for a wonderful two weeks in Panama. I loved swimming in the ocean and tried (unsuccessfully) to teach Marla to body surf in the warm Pacific. We visited montane Parque Nacional Omar Torrijos and walked in some of the hardest rain imaginable, looking for the endangered and mysterious Panamanian golden frog on the Sendero La Rana Dorada trail. We just laughed about how wet we got despite our fancy rain gear! Sadly, we did not see a golden frog.

When we stayed in Portobelo on the Caribbean side, I noticed that all the septic systems in the area were at sea level. I surmised that when the tide rose, the septic tanks might fill, and when the tide went out, some of the septic tank contents probably went out into the bay. I wasn't sure, but since there was no way to test it, I decided not to swim in the local bay. However, Marla dismissed my assessment and had a nice little swim out to the Black Jesus statue in the center of the bay. The pictures I took were gorgeous. Of course, some water got in her mouth on the swim. Twelve hours later, she regretted her decision, but we had lots of toilet paper and meds available, so she recovered in a day or two.

After this interlude on the Caribbean coast, we caught the regular local bus back to the Colon train depot. Our bus driver advised us not to walk into town – too dangerous. Heeding his advice, we took a cab from the depot into town to the best restaurant (per the driver); it was called 'Madonna's' by the locals. Sweet. Upon arriving, we learned that the actual spelling was McDonalds! Not what we were hoping for. Nearing departure time for the train back to Panama City, we took our chances and walked the ten blocks back to the depot. In due time, the train came in, and we enjoyed a glass of wine while riding in restored Pullman cars on the tracks that parallel the Panama Canal.

Another one of our expeditions involved driving my venerable jeep, Nellie Belle, on some gnarly old mining roads that tourists in Death Valley are warned to avoid (I have some special maps of the area that we consulted). We had a week of near solitude in the depths of one of America's most amazing national parks and the surrounding public lands. Old Nellie never let us down, and we visited hot springs, bathtubs filled with blue marbles and yellow rubber ducks (Steele Pass), old gold mines and ghost towns, and abandoned ranches. We dined al fresco with wild burros and coyotes and enjoyed magnificent stars and the Milky Way at night.

Alas, all good things must end, or at least change. While Marla was out west, gallivanting around in the mountains with me, her

Waco veterinary clinic was in slow decline. She had been gone most of three years, with her clinic staffed by a relief vet, and clients started to drift away to other doctors. Over some months, Marla came to realize that her clinic was going to dry up like one of those desert ghost towns if she did not get herself back to Waco full time. She left in the summer of 2013, and I carried on with my work. We missed each other a lot - thank goodness for cell phones with unlimited minutes.

Marla owned a 1930 Craftsman-style stone house that she called Hound Haven, which was rented to Baylor college students at the time. Her sister and brother-in-law have a large house on five acres near Cameron Park in NE Waco, so Marla decamped to the largely unused back wing of their house. I flew out a couple of times to visit, and her family gave me a warm welcome. That was a huge relief, as not getting along with one's future spouse's family is a rough road. And yes, I had it in my mind that I wanted to marry this girl.

In October, I broached the subject over dinner at my house in Fresno. Specifically, I asked her what kind of wedding ring she would like, IF she could have one. She gave me a strange look: Where was I going with this question? We discussed the virtues of platinum, titanium, molybdenum, gold, and silver. We quickly dismissed gold and silver as metals too soft for active people - the ring would be damaged by rock climbing and such. We got on the computer after dinner and looked at the stronger metals. I told her that I wanted to buy her a wedding ring, and make her my bride, and she said that molybdenum looked promising. I ordered us a set of rings to 'try on for size.' Soon, I had her wearing a ring as a test.

Marla and I had both been married before. However, when we met, we had been single for a decade. We both had financial problems in our former marriages, and although we were madly in love, we were also gun-shy about marrying again. Marla was saddled with a lot of debt after her first marriage ended, and she was certainly not willing to go there again. I am allergic to credit card debt and can live on beans and rice if needed to keep the bank account in the black. So, we had fiscal conservatism in common.

Doing my ultimate best as a salesman, I convinced her to elope with me to Reno at the very end of 2013, to marry for better or worse. Marla chose a drive-through chapel for us. Arriving there after a long night of driving, we found the drive-through wedding area blocked with snow. We went inside, bought some flowers for the photos, and were married by a very wise, kind, elderly man who gave me some excellent advice: "Your job is to make your wife happy." Think about that for a moment. It's as obvious as the sky is blue that no one can *make* another person happy.

What I took him to mean was that there was a lot I could do to ease my wife's daily struggles. So, I have tried to take his sage advice to heart every day. To this end, I consciously wake up next to her in a good mood. I am playful. I bring her a cup of fresh-ground coffee each day as she reposes in bed. I do her laundry. I make her delicious dinners. I surprise her with flowers, and chocolates, and sparkling wine. I listen when she has a bad day. I take her on tandem bicycle rides and do most of the pedaling. I tell her that she is beautiful and nibble her ear as often as possible. For these life skills, I wish to thank any woman I ever dated in the past who trained me in some way.

After a bit of skiing in the Sierra at the New Year holiday, we took off in my old Subaru WRX toward Texas. I thought it would be fun to visit a few national parks on the way (it's in my DNA). First, we drove across Nevada to Zion National Park in SW Utah. Zion can be a bit stark and bleak in winter, but also very beautiful with super clear air and the sun, low in the sky, casting big shadows on all the mountain ranges. Although it was cold at night, we had some fun daytime hikes in the park on uncrowded trails. Leaving Zion, we cut across northern Arizona, traversing Indian country, visiting Navajo stores, and buying locally-grown blue corn masa and Anasazi beans. We visited little thrift stores in small towns, finding treasures among the debris of randomly donated goods. Our honeymoon trip was a giant, rolling treasure hunt.

Once we left the western mountains, we pushed on to Waco. I enjoyed a few sweet nights with my bride in the 'newlywed wing' at her sister's house, and then flew back to Fresno. While married and very happy, I was also slightly miserable being away from my beloved wife. I needed to join her in Waco permanently, and as soon as possible.

After our wedding and Marla's return to Waco, her clinic was a success, and she was quite busy. Her staff did a big push on social media to announce that Dr. Marla was back full time, and her clients responded. Her sister and brother-in-law gave her great support and always welcomed me when I was able to fly out for a long weekend. Marla came out West to ski with me for a few weekends, too, but we both looked forward to me joining her in Waco permanently. This meant giving up a great teaching job at Cal Poly San Luis Obispo, but it was worth any sacrifice to be with her.

I started to plan my exit strategy. The steps were to finish the school year in June, sell my house in Fresno, and get myself to Waco soon thereafter. When I told my university department chair that I was leaving, he was understanding, but also concerned. I was teaching some original classes in air quality. Because the field is specialized, my department chairman asked me to help him find a replacement. Fortunately, I had been taking my students to the Conoco-Phillips refinery in Arroyo Grande for several years, and I knew the environmental manager well. He had an advanced degree and was interested in teaching at Cal Poly. I helped prepare him for an interview and he was able to take over my classes without missing a beat. Exit goal #1 completed.

Next, I had to find a buyer for the Fresno house that I had inherited from my dad. I had an ace in the hole that made this house special. Allow me to explain. Fresno has very low rainfall – something like 11" per year. Water comes from snowmelt in the Sierra Nevada mountains through a system of canals and ditches. These canals are connected to a wide network of ponds specifically built to recharge groundwater.

Right behind my house was a large groundwater recharge pond. My dad had a 6-foot-high wooden palisade fence in the backyard, so he never saw the reservoir. When I took over, that fence came down, providing a nice water view from the living room and back deck. Moreover, the deck faced west, so the house enjoyed some of the most magnificent sunsets I have ever seen. As a bonus, Canada geese liked the pond in winter. I spent one spring feeding birdseed to a gaggle of goslings, helping mama and papa goose raise the little guys. This water view was a big selling point.

    My house was also energy efficient with lots of passive daylighting along with solar tubes and photovoltaic panels. With California's graduated electric rates, staying in the lowest price tier with solar makes huge financial sense. This would save the potential homebuyer several hundred dollars a month on their electric bill. Buyers appreciate this potential savings, especially when it can help them make their monthly house payments. Because the house had new floors, fresh paint, and the energy improvements, it sold for the asking price after just five days on the market. Ka-ching! Exit goal #2 completed. Finally, I planned the actual move to Waco and my lovely bride.

Chapter 2   The Search

Waco's Cameron Park is a unique urban gem. It was founded about 120 years ago along the banks of the Brazos River, and has become a mecca for mountain biking, hiking and trail running. Cameron Park is one of the largest urban parks in the United States and many people would love to live near it. Many homes near the park are sold by word-of-mouth because the area is so popular. Because Marla is an avid runner who trains on the trails in Waco's Cameron Park, and we both enjoy cycling, we were committed to finding a house nearby where we could hit the trails right out the back door.

Cameron Park is a rugged area of limestone bluffs about 200 feet high above the confluence of the Brazos and Bosque rivers. The park has been expanded and developed over time to have very nice picnic areas along both sides of the Brazos River, with about 20 miles of rugged trails upland from the water. In the past 20 years, mountain bikers have maintained and nurtured the trails, and they are shared by many hikers and runners. When I met Marla, she had already completed half a dozen tough 100-mile running races, and she used the trails of Cameron Park extensively to stay fit for the next race.

There is also a neighborhood called Cameron Park, which comprises large brick and stone estate homes surrounded by massive lawns dotted with oaks. Some neighbors, in contrast, often live in small wood frame homes with modest yards. This neighborhood has five acre lots mixed in with 1/8 acre lots. Marla and I could not afford a big estate home, while the small frame homes that were for sale needed a ton of work. Importantly for us, there was no beauty in many of the smaller homes, no emotional connection. We were eventually able to find a house (built by the Mailanders) in the Brook Oaks neighborhood, next door to Cameron Park, and just two blocks from the Brazos River Trail that leads to the dirt running trails Marla trains on.

When Marla and I were married in late December 2013, we planned for me to continue my teaching job until June 2014 and then move to be with her in Waco. Marla wanted to find us a house to share for our new marriage. However, I was still working 1,600 miles away in California so I wasn't much help in the search. We knew that we wanted to live near the Brazos River and Cameron Park, but that was about it. Marla had free rein in her house searching – I had confidence in her.

Marla spent a lot of time with her sister, Gail, and brother-in-law, Dan, looking at houses that might be our first home together. Dan is a 30-year career Army officer who was transferred frequently. Consequently, Gail (who was on the *Fixer Upper* show with Marla) had bought and sold many houses and knows real estate well. We were lucky, as Gail was a big asset for house-hunting. Marla also enlisted her friend Greta who lived in and had a pulse on the Cameron Park neighborhood.

Marla describes the situation:

After I returned to my practice full time, I had been living in Waco for about three months in my sister Gail's house. She has a large estate-like house with a whole wing that was rarely occupied until I took up residence. So, I did have plenty of room, but still at the age of 50-something, it just didn't seem right to live in the back portion of my sister and her husband's house. Therefore, I was on a perpetual search for housing. Dave was still living in Fresno in the house that he had acquired from his father and done some remodeling on, but we were without housing in Waco. I owned an old stone house called Hound Haven, but it was rented long-term to a group of college students. Plus, that house is not close to Cameron Park.

My route to work each day from my sister's house, in the Cameron Park neighborhood, took me down 5th Street, which is one-way. Every day I would pass by an older, kind of dilapidated house on the left side. Sometime around February/March a 'For Sale' sign appeared in the yard. Finally, I got enough courage up to call my real estate agent, Doug Eastland, to see if we could visit the house. I took my sister and her husband along to see the house. Doug just happened to work for Magnolia Realty. I believe he was their only *agent at the time* [which explains why it was easy for him to contact Chip].

We went in the house and looked around – the structure had some nice built-in cabinets and lots of windows, but it was obviously derelict with a lot of debris in the house. The outside was scary with neglect as well. There were some nice things about the house, such as high ceilings and big windows that provided lots of light. It had three fireplaces and hardwood floors that were somewhat visible. These things made the house very attractive to me. It had a feeling of something that could be turned around.

Doug, who understood my interest in older houses since this was the fifth house we had toured, realized that this house was a possible candidate for purchase. The houses I looked at needed to be under $50,000 in an area adjacent to Cameron Park and not impossible to remodel. While I was looking at this house, thinking to myself, if only I knew how to fix this house up, it would be great, the real estate agent was saying, 'This house would be perfect for the last episode of Fixer Upper.*'*

I wasn't sure what Fixer Upper *was; I hadn't seen the show. At that time, the show had not gained much momentum. It was only Season 1, and most people, (including, as I learned, the lending institutions in the area) thought it would be a flash-in-the-pan and over soon. So, my problem was that I could not quite imagine how I could take this house and turn it into something that would work for me. During this time, walking through the property, Doug persisted in saying that he was sure this house would be a perfect candidate for* Fixer Upper *and he would call Chip Gaines and talk to him right away.*

So, he made the call, and within fifteen minutes, Chip was getting out of the truck - literally in his work clothes, tool belt, the whole thing, with no TV cameras in sight, bounding up the steps looking at the house and saying, 'This is absolutely perfect.' He was simply the most enthusiastic person I have ever met. He said, 'No problem. $35,000, buy it for $35,000, put 40 into it, maybe 55 – 60, all in, $90,000 total. We can do it.'

I had never heard of <u>Fixer Upper</u>, or Chip and Joanna Gaines. Fortunately, my office manager, Dotti, was one of those who followed the show and Joanna's blog. She was part of a group of people who wanted to make their houses 'homier' with a decorating style. Dotti felt that any house that Chip and Joanna remodeled would be a good investment. Dotti said that I would never regret it, and she was willing to do all the on-the-ground work to make a remodel happen.

When Chip came in and spoke with Doug, the real estate agent, we found out the house was being sold by a gentleman, Mr. C, who lived up the street. The sale was a little confusing because there were a lot of personal items inside, and we were not sure if they were going to be sold along with the house. I initially thought that Mr. C had inherited the house from his grandmother's estate. Because we were very interested in the house and wanted to know its history, I was really looking forward to meeting Mr. C. And he was also a picker and his father had been a picker. [A picker is a local colloquial name for someone who goes to estate sales and knows what items have resale value].

Mr. C was a delightful gentleman and so I was sure I would learn a whole lot about the history of the house. When Doug called him, much to my surprise. Mr. C came right over. We walked through the house and he told me what items he would remove if we did not want them. I like old books; he said, 'You can keep those.' We had a nice conversation and I asked if this was his grandmother's house and he said, 'No, no, I live in my grandmother's house.' I was a little bit confused and said, 'I thought this was your grandmother's house.' He said, 'No, no, my grandmother's house was moved from Austin Avenue to Fifth Street. She worked for a man who lived on Austin Avenue for years and when he wanted to move a turn-of-the-century frame house from his property, he offered it to her, and he moved it to Fifth St., so she could live there.' And that is where Mr. C was living, about three blocks up, in his mother's house."

I said, 'So what do you know about this house?' Mr. C is a wealth of information, and he said, 'Well, my father bought it from an old gentleman who had bought it from the Mailanders.' The man he bought it from had rented it to college students who were artists. Some of the things like the outdoor fireplace in the backyard were probably student art projects. We were never sure what was added by others after the last Mailander passed, but the most interesting thing was a memory Mr. C had. He did remember the original owners of the house [probably Wilhelmina Mailander Henjes, who would have been an elderly woman at the time, as she died in 1961]. Mr. C said that he and his older brother and other kids would run down the block from his grandmother's house on the sidewalk. He said she [the elderly woman] would be sweeping the porch and she spoke English with a thick German accent, and she chased them off when they were rambunctiously trying to explore her yard. [According to her death certificate, Mrs. Henjes was born in Germany in 1880 and immigrated to the United States as an infant with her parents.]

Now here is the same story from Dotti's perspective:

"My name is Dotti Bolen and I am the manager at Crossroads Animal Clinic in Waco, Texas, and these are just a few samples from my experience working with Marla Hendricks and her <u>Fixer Upper</u> house, later referred to as the Mailander House.

I was involved in some capacity during all stages of the process. From the initial tour of the property, to the paperwork involved in participating on the show, to the design efforts and final reveal. It was truly a fascinating experience!

As Marla Hendrick's hospital manager/personal assistant, I first toured the Mailander House with a local realtor, Doug, who we have used for many real estate purchases in the Waco area. At the time, Doug was working for Magnolia Realty, and as we toured the house, he looked at me and stated this would be a great house for 'the show.' I agreed as I had already seen several episodes that had aired on HGTV. I explained the concept to Dr. Hendricks and encouraged her to take this once-in-a-lifetime opportunity. Doug called Chip to come look at the house, and they decided that they did want to pursue this property for the show. And that is how the ball started rolling.

My next experience was the day that Joanna walked through the property and came up with her design plan. They asked me to be present since I knew Marla, and hopefully what she would and would not like. We toured the property again. It was fascinating watching Joanna and her design team work. She very quickly came up with her plan, which walls would come down, the features that she would maintain the integrity of, and how she would go about it.

The night before the 'big reveal,' I received a phone call from Joanna's assistant, Lindsey. They were at the house, staging everything for the next day's reveal and filming, when they saw a vehicle that looked like Marla's driving by the house. They called me to see if I could go sit on her and make sure that she wasn't trying to get a sneak peek before reveal day. Turns out, it was not Marla but a similar car in the neighborhood. That next morning, I went to Marla's house to make sure she showed up for filming on time. I followed Marla and Dave to the meeting spot with Chip and Joanna a short distance from the house. From that point on, I watched from a distance as the filming took place." (Dotti took photos with her cell phone of filming 'the reveal' from across the street - included in this book).

Chapter 3   The Neighborhood

One of our activities when I visited Waco was to walk all the streets in the Cameron Park neighborhood to look at houses. There were a few good ones for sale and there were a few real dogs. One house that I liked a lot was a single-story Mid-Century Modern shaded by numerous mature oaks. It had a separate garage perfect for a bike workroom and to store toys such as kayaks and canoes. This Mid-Century house looked good and was priced right – they were asking just $110,000.

We had a chance to look inside and some of the charm wore off quickly. First, the lovely hardwood floors had a pronounced tilt in the front room. The room probably slanted two or three inches from the center of the house toward the outside. A few of the bedrooms and the adjoining bath were very dark. The kitchen underwhelmed – it reminded me of a room for people who don't cook but feel they must have something. And finally, there were several good-sized oaks growing right next to the slab foundation and cracking the sidewalks. Although the location was prime, this house would certainly need some work.

I told Marla to go for it and start bidding. She came in low, but in the meantime, another person came in at the full asking price of $110,000 and the house sold. We learned the hard way that even houses needing serious work in the Cameron Park neighborhood sell quickly. (An acquaintance of ours bought the house in 2014 and completed many of the needed repairs and upgrades. He then sold it to another of our friends in 2017 who are very happy with their home.)

Our next bid was on a neglected frame house down the hill on 5th St (which we subsequently learned was built by Fred Mailander). This house was old but had some good features, and the asking price was about $45,000 (it turned out we bought it for less than $40,000, including paying the previous year's taxes). It was on 1/3 acre with several mature trees. It had large covered porches on the south and west sides. It had high ceilings with many, many windows. It had three fireplaces with nice masonry work, and the entire house was clad in hardwood floors. I did an extensive visual inspection under and around the house, and the flooring timbers and exposed wood on the outside all appeared to be free of water damage or termites. However, the neighborhood was doubtful at first glance.

Much of Waco's early settlement was on the east side of the Brazos River. Major floods encouraged those who could afford a lot on higher ground to the west, to build there. Mailander House, on the west side of the river, is well above the maximum high-water level ever recorded. One hundred twenty years ago, the area along North 4th and 5th streets was a prime residential location and many prominent families built in the area. As desegregation became the law of the land, many white Waco families tended to move west and north, leaving the original neighborhoods behind. By the 1980s, the Mailander House neighborhood was scary – folks who grew up here had stories of shootings and violence. In the minds of some locals, nothing has changed since then – which of course is not true since there has been tremendous progress in the past 40 years.

There is an axiom in real estate sales: location, location, location. Practically speaking, this means that one can have the nicest house in the world, but it won't sell for much if the locale is bad (traffic, noise, crime, smells from a hog lot next door, etc.). The location of the Mailander House on 5th St. was a bit dubious to me. It was obvious that this part of Waco had been settled for a long time, but there were many empty lots where houses once stood. Walking around nearby, we found half a dozen empty houses where the owners had died and the home was wasting away like John Brown's body. The sidewalks were either missing or in disrepair. I saw large City of Waco utility trucks going up and down Indiana St., which faces the south side of the house. I thought, "So much for sitting on the porches and enjoying a quiet cup of coffee." Later, I was proved wrong, as the city trucks only drive that way when the workers are done for the day, about 3:30, but this was my first impression and influenced my early feelings about the location.

As we looked at the house, I started doing my 'Chip Gaines assessment' - what will it take to fix this place? The house itself had some real problems. First off, the roof was in bad shape and would need immediate refurbishing. Water was not coming into the house - yet. There were several large trees growing very close to the side of the house. These provided nice shade, but were a danger in high winds, and of course the roots could play hell with a foundation (more about that later). The back part of the house appeared to be an add-on for a bathroom and laundry and this area's foundation was obviously shot. The basement was unlocked, and I went under the house, looking at the plumbing and wiring. They were both very old and would need immediate replacement. The heating/air conditioning system was gone. The kitchen was a joke. No wonder the asking price was so low.

However, the general location was good for our lifestyle. The house was just two blocks from the Brazos River Trail. It is one flat mile along the river trail to the Redwood Shelter where many running and mountain bike events begin. Also, proximity to downtown was good, and it would be very easy to ride a bike to any number of restaurants and shops. Best of all was the price, which was within our budget. We decided to go for it. Initially I thought I would have to do all the work, but the interest shown by Chip in filming the repair and remodel really clinched the deal for us. Not only would we have the work done by licensed contractors, but we would also have the project completed quickly.

Marla tells a story:

The first time I met Chip Gaines, I had just walked through the house that would become Episode 13 in Season One of <u>Fixer Upper</u>. *As I described in Chapter 1, Chip was very enthusiastic about remodeling this house on the* <u>Fixer Upper</u> *TV show. But before I ever met Chip, his realtor had been working with me for several months. When we first looked at the Mailander House, Doug Eastland, my long-suffering realtor, said, 'You know this could be the final episode of* <u>Fixer Upper</u> *this year. There are other houses that owners would like to have remodeled on* <u>Fixer Upper</u>, *but none that are as good as this one.' I call Doug Eastland 'long- suffering' because he had done a lot of work to help me find a house* [now called Hound Haven] *seven years earlier. I have always had an affinity for old houses that* were built around the turn of the 20th century, have hardwood floors, and finally and most importantly, are inexpensive.

This was something like the fifth house Doug and I had looked at in five months. The first house, though small, was about a mile from Cameron Park and listed for $36,000. Doug thought I could offer less, since he had to inform me as a matter of real estate law, that a death had occurred on the property. I was not deterred as people die every day in hospitals, on highways and yes, sometimes at home. Doug said, 'Actually on this occasion it was homicide.' Still thinking it might not be that bad, I asked, 'Drive-by shooting?' Doug answered, 'Nope, beaten to death in the front yard.' 'Oh,' I said, 'Let's offer $16,000.' Thankfully that offer was too low and someone else bought that house. A series of similar episodes followed.

I made a few offers and paid for inspections to be done. Doug called me after one of the houses was inspected and announced, 'Good news on this one, the doorbell passed inspection.' I said, 'What about the rest of the property?' Doug said, 'Nope, just the doorbell.' So, this is where we were, and honestly, the house we wound up buying was pretty rough on the inside. Yes, it was a corner lot and the house had hardwood floors and amazing windows and three fireplaces, but the roof was old and starting to leak, and the plumbing had long ago stopped functioning. Nothing in this house would pass inspection and there was a lot of stuff just left all over the house. It would take a lot of optimism to see light in this tunnel and that is where Chip entered the scene.

Chip is charismatic; he could sell ice cubes to Eskimos. He is unpretentious and relentlessly optimistic. I met Chip the first day that we looked at the house, then again when the financing problems happened and he brought his friend the Loan Fish, and there was not another meeting that was not documented on TV until I met him over tea and cupcakes at the house after we had moved in.

Just about the time we were closing on the house, Marla threw me a curve ball. It turned out to be a huge blessing, although we did not know it at the time. Marla and I spent many hours each week talking on the phone since we could not be together physically. On one of our evening calls, Marla asked me if I would be okay with a TV reality show remodeling our new house on 5th St. My first reaction was, "Absolutely yes!" (with some reservations that I did not voice at the time). I knew first-hand how much work it is to remodel a beat-down house. Even if we could hire contractors for the heavy lifting work, there would still be a ton of small details for the owner/remodeler (me) to attend to, endless hours tracking down bids for labor and materials, and trips to Home Depot. Because I did not know any contractors in Waco, finding the good ones would certainly be a greenhorn's challenge.

Here is how lady luck shone her light upon us: As Marla has related, she was doing a final walk through at our new house to close the sale when our real estate agent, Doug Eastland with Magnolia Realty, casually asked if we would be interested in having the home repaired by a TV show. Marla said, "Sure, but what's involved?" In early 2014, the first season of *Fixer Upper* had only been on the air for about five programs, and the producers were in a time crunch to wrap the filming of the first season.

The *Fixer Upper* production team needed to film one more episode to finish up for the year, and they were under the gun to get it done very quickly. Chip had been looking at houses to remodel for the final TV episode and had found a rather boring potential remodel in the suburbs, but he was still looking for something more dramatic. He really wanted to show his chops in a powerful and beautiful conclusion to the first season's work. He was only at the Mailander House for five minutes before he enthusiastically declared that he wanted this house for the show.

Part II Fixer-Upper Unleashed

Chapter 4 What It Takes to Be a Fixer Upper

Buying an old house that needs a lot of work can be scary because the project may not turn out well. Some days working on the house may feel like the wheels are spinning with no forward motion. Also, to complete a big remodel project requires confidence and an ability to overcome obstacles and persevere. Generally, bankers do not like to loan on speculative projects-- this could be called "institutional fear." It may be necessary to find creative funding options (which can mean higher interest rates).

One primary reason many older homes are not restored is that people do not have confidence and courage. To work on an old house, one cannot give up when the going gets tough. As a youth, I was strongly influenced by the ideas of the Outward Bound program. The motto of the original Outward Bound was "To serve, to strive and not to yield." Outward Bound was originally founded in 1941 to increase the survival chances of young seamen whose ships were torpedoed in the mid-Atlantic. It seems that sailors were giving up hope early; if they could just hold on, they could be rescued. The Outward Bound mental training, to persevere, saved many lives.

To some degree, the buyers of the 'left for dead' Mailander House had to be people who would persevere. They needed to be without fear of either the work, the money spent, or the neighborhood. Why Marla and I are these people is a major theme of this book. Objective fear, for me, usually meant overcoming demons in my mind (such as childhood fear of the dark) or a physical threat to life, such as falling while rock climbing. Taking on a big remodeling home project has a different kind of fear that must also be confronted and overcome.

When it was first presented to me, I was a bit dubious about this offer to be on TV. I asked who Chip was, and Marla said that he was known around town as someone who 'flipped' houses. What this means is that the flipper buys a distressed property, slaps some paint on everything, maybe does a little bathroom/kitchen work and then resells the house quickly. The whole idea is to be in-and-out fast, so the money turns over. Ideally, the flipper has a real estate license and makes money on the sales fees too. When Marla relayed this to me, I felt this was a dubious option. But she persisted with her usual upbeat outlook and testified that the TV show crew would not be doing a 'flipper job' but a real proper remodel. She also verified that Magnolia had a pretty good team of craftsmen who knew how to remodel according to the building codes.

I wondered if this work would pass muster if we wanted to sell the house down the road. Marla asserted that Magnolia would give us a bonafide contract for the remodel that included a complete re-roofing, re-plumbing, foundation repair, rewiring, completely new kitchen, bathroom remodeling, stripping and restoring the hardwood floors, installing a heating/cooling system, and painting the entire house inside and out. This all sounded great to me; the problem was that we did not have $65,000 lying around right then. When I sold my house in Fresno we would, but that was still four months away.

I had been consistently working 10-12-hour days, either at Cal Poly San Luis Obispo, where I was teaching, or working on my Dad's old house in Fresno. Consequently, I rarely watched TV, although I was aware of home repair shows. I also had a three-hour, 160 mile commute each way every week between Fresno and San Luis Obispo which chewed up some time. My concern in having a TV show do the work was that flippers often cover up serious problems (like water damage and mold) with paint and Fix-It-All (a plaster material that is often used to repair interiors). My motto when buying any home from a flipper is 'caveat emptor,' or 'Let the buyer beware.' I wanted to learn more about these Magnolia people before I agreed to get in bed with them, so to speak.

The TV producers also wanted to learn more about us, and they had Marla fill out a questionnaire, part of which is shown below (her responses are in italics):

Tell us about your home search. How many homes have you looked at? Please describe all the homes that you have looked at and why they have not worked for you.

I have looked at seven houses. HOUSE ONE: The first house had a good location on a corner lot and had been updated but was outside my price range and needed foundation repair.

HOUSE TWO: This house was in my price range but would have required major renovations. It also suffered from a lack of character and inadequate lot size.

HOUSE THREE: This house was in my price range but would have needed major repairs which would have used up any funds that could be used to remodel. The lot size was also inadequate.

HOUSE FOUR: The fourth house was inhabited but uninhabitable due to renters that had misused the property and were still living in the house. It was scary!

HOUSE FIVE: In and below my price range but the neighborhood was not safe, and the structure was unsound.

HOUSE SIX: Was a beautiful house but way outside of my price range and would have required an additional $50,000 in repairs.

Tell us about the home you are most interested in – What do you love about it, what do you dislike about it. Why would you say this is the right location but wrong house?

HOUSE SEVEN: It has a beautiful corner lot in the right neighborhood. This house is close to the park and in an area that is undergoing active revitalization. The basic design of the house is very pleasing, and I can envision it being my next home. It is currently a mix between Mission Style and Victorian features. I would like the renovations to reflect a more Urban Cottage style.

If you do buy this home, why are you willing to live with this home's deficiencies?

This home has tons of authentic charm, it has historic features that I would like to see refurbished, and it is in the exact location I have been wanting.

If someone were to build you a dream home - please describe what your dream home would be like.

I would love a small cottage-style home with high ceilings and open spaces that connect. It needs to be functional for living and entertaining. The house should open onto the porches and lawn in such a way that there is a connection between the kitchen and kitchen garden.

Talking about the home you are considering purchasing, if we could help you turn this home into your dream home, what would it look like? Please be descriptive (feel free to send tear sheets of things you've dreamt of for the space).

I would like to maintain the footprint of the house. I would like for the French doors and fireplaces to remain. I would like to repurpose/reuse as much of the original material as possible. I would like for the kitchen, dining room and porch to blend. The kitchen would be warm and inviting with functional work space and a gas stove. The bedrooms and bathrooms would be tranquil. I want the hardwood floors throughout to be refurbished. No carpeting because I want a pet-friendly environment. An appropriate area for reading with lots of natural light would be ideal.

Plumbing, foundation, rewiring, and central heat and air are my first priorities. Most important renovations would be to make two bathrooms and the kitchen functional. I would also like to preserve the rock wall outside and the stone structure in the backyard and make it a part of the final plans, if possible. I would also like to keep the basement. The existing shed could become my husband's bicycle workshop.

Describe your design style. If your mate's design style differs from yours, please elaborate.

Repurposed vintage cottage. My husband's style is the same.

What are your turn ons/turn offs when it comes to design and your home?

Turn ons – eclectic style, maintaining the authenticity of the house. I like the simplicity of natural materials brought indoors.

Turn offs – clutter, over decorating. I dislike store-bought design.

Do you have any 'dream projects' or elements you envision for your home?

Here are a few ideas: A library area with a reading nook, a functional farm kitchen, an organic garden, a romantic bedroom, a bedroom that is functional so that our altitude tent and stationary bike can fit.

Is there anything 'off limits'? Are you willing to have us rewire, rip down walls, etc.?

Off limits – Fireplaces, French doors, original windows. I have no problems with moving walls.

Tell us about your favorite stores.

Restoration Hardware, Restore, LL Bean, Honey's Homestyle

How would this change you and your family's lives?

The help you would give us in design and moving the renovation process forward would be invaluable because of the time savings. This would enable me to focus on my full time, six day a week veterinary practice and allow my husband to relocate to Waco, Texas. We would also be able to focus on our hobbies, and could start our married life together in Waco instead of constant commuting and a long-distance relationship!

When it comes to the design of your home, i.e. where things will be installed, placed, etc. our show will take your thoughts into consideration, but FINAL DETERMINATION OF THE DESIGN RESTS WITH THE SHOW'S DESIGNERS AND PRODUCERS. After an initial discussion with our designer, you will NOT be able to have any further contact with our design team. Are you willing to trust our expertise and hand over TOTAL control of this renovation to the HGTV experts?

YES

What is the financial amount you can contribute to this renovation?

$40,000

So that was the gist of the questions the production company asked on our first go-round. Marla's estimate for how much it would cost to do all the work was extremely optimistic. As she asserted in the Prologue, she pulls numbers out of "her air." Honestly, maybe she thought the TV show would kick in money for all the rest of the work - $40,000 was not going to go very far.

The Magnolia budget that Joanna prepared came in looking like this:

New electrical	$8,500
Redo Flooring	$3,000
Kitchen Update	$17,000
Install new cabinets	
Countertops	
Backsplash	
Hardware	
Plumbing & Electrical	
Sheetrock repair/interior paint	$8,000
Bathroom flooring/paint updates	$3,000
Exterior wall repair and paint	$6,000
New roof	$7,500
Level house	$1,500
New central heat and air	$5,500
Plumbing upgrade	<u>$5,000</u>
Total	**$65,000**

The Magnolia remodel budget did not include kitchen appliances, so we budgeted another $5,000 for these. There was no point in going cheap, so we got Kenmore Elite products and have never regretted it.

Because the TV producers were in a real hurry to get the filming started, we had to come up with $65,000 fast, which was more money than we had on hand. Marla has had a successful veterinary practice in Waco for over 20 years. She has a half-dozen employees and operates a regular animal hospital with expensive diagnostic equipment and a full gamut of animal drugs and treatments. She has used the same commercial bank for years, running the payroll and operation costs through the local bank branch. Logically, she called her banker and asked him for a home improvement loan. We owned the property outright and thought this should be a slam-dunk.

Chapter 5   The Loan Fish

When Marla's long-time banker came over to look at the house to evaluate our loan request, no work had started yet. It was full of junk and old furniture from the lady who had passed on while living there, and her son had not yet cleaned it out (the pictures tell the story). The ceiling was falling in part of the living room, and the yard was full of weeds. The house was on the city tax rolls appraised at $58,000. We told the banker that we had $34,000 in it (not including the back taxes we paid separately) and wanted to spend another $65,000. He did not see how that was going to make sense – we would be underwater about $40,000 (compared to the tax assessment). He did not like the neighborhood, and flat out refused to lend on the house remodeling. We took a deep breath, and Marla told *Fixer Upper* we could not come up with the money.

Chip almost immediately came to the rescue with a Loan Fish (not a Loan Shark)! In Chip's work flipping houses, he often used banks to help purchase homes, and sometimes had multiple houses undergoing renovation or for sale at the same time. Sometimes when his credit limit was reached at the bank, he used local people with available cash to help finance properties. If Chip found a screaming deal but had no cash, he would go fishing for money – and when he caught a lender, he called that person a Loan Fish. Chip had such a lender for us, but the rates were not pretty.

At Marla's initial meeting, the Loan Fish and his attorney proposed an interest-only loan with no term limit. Marla, playing dumb, asked sweetly, "So when will the loan be paid off?" The Loan Fish and attorney both looked down at the table and said that the interest-only payments would not pay off the loan EVER. Then, the Loan Fish and his attorney got serious and proposed a 15-year note at 10%. Marla countered, and we finally agreed to a $65,000, two-year note at 10% simple interest. There was no penalty for early payoff.

This meant that we had to repay or refinance the house in two years, and the Loan Fish held the property deed in case we defaulted. It was risky because of the low property assessment (before the remodel), but we wanted the house ready to live in as soon as possible, so we said, "Yes!" I also believed that I was going to come out OK selling the house in Fresno. This is where Marla and I are in accord: We accept risk, just like following an unknown rock-climbing route. In climbing, we often start at the bottom without being able to see the summit, while trusting in our ability to succeed.

Marla remembers:

The fun happened when it came down to Thursday at 4 PM, and our banker called and said, 'Marla can borrow money, but not on that house. <u>Fixer Upper</u> is unproven, Chip and Joanna Gaines try to do a lot of things, but we don't know how that's going. We cannot fund the $65,000 [remodel cost] *plus the $35,000* [purchase price] *which is $100,000. Even with 20% down, she will have to provide us with CDs up to $30,000. In addition, we can consider a $50,000 loan if she puts down $50,000 in CDs plus cash in our bank.'*

Well, that wasn't going to happen in the next 24 hours, so we called our real estate agent, Doug, who worked for Magnolia Realty, and said, 'We regret to inform you that our bank will not fund this project.' When our real estate agent took the news to Chip, Chip said, 'No problem, we can find you someone to loan the money.' I said, 'Good. I'm at work and I'm busy. Let me know how this works out.' Chip said, 'How about 10 o'clock tomorrow? I have two friends who will make this happen.' The next morning, I was introduced to a lovely gentleman who was investing his ailing father's money in good real estate projects.

The great thing about it was Mr. Loan Fish brought his attorney friend, who was a numbers man, and he was able to offer us an interest-only note for two years. Or, if we really wanted to get ahead in the game, we could have a 30-year rate mortgage [where payments are almost all interest with very little toward principal] *with the balloon payoff after two years. So, my choices were interest-only, or 30-year fixed with the balloon payment at the end of two years. It was a busy day in my clinic, and I didn't have a mortgage calculator handy, so I asked, 'Just let me be sure I understand. I can have either one of two options: a 30-year* *mortgage or an interest-only mortgage, and I can pay $3,000 for the loan origination fee and at the end of two years I will have paid no principal on my home. There's only a slight difference in the first two years between interest-only and 30-years fixed, so it's really minor.'*

I enjoyed the look of amazement on the face of the attorney who was handling the paperwork when I said, 'Why would anyone do that?' What followed was some stammering about how some people don't really care how they spend their money and they need to pay interest for a long, long, time, and then I said, 'How would you feel about a note with a 15-year rate, [where a lot more of the loan principal can be paid early] *with a balloon at the end of two years? And the attorney sort of opened his eyes wide and said, 'Well obviously, financially, that is the best choice.' And that's what we did.*

The Loan Fish turned out to be a nice guy with an interesting story of his own. He had come to Waco about 30 years before and had started a small carpet-cleaning business with borrowed money. He would clean carpets anytime, anywhere, and he did most of the work himself. Our Loan Fish also started cleaning and painting apartments before they were re-rented. With Baylor University and the other smaller colleges constantly graduating and then adding new students, there is a frequent turnover of apartments. This guy had hit a small gold mine, but he had to do the physical work himself for it to pay off.

Our Loan Fish wisely started using his profits to invest in rental properties. Over time, he had amassed several apartment buildings and large commercial properties that provided a tidy income. He also made private loans at above market rates to people like us, creating another nice little revenue stream for himself. To his credit, he still cleans and repairs many of these properties himself when needed. And, to make our deal with him even sweeter, he was super nice to me and let me sit in his Maserati when he came by one day; those leather seats are so comfortable!

As a final note to this chapter, after two years, we had paid down a substantial amount of the loan and were able to refinance at the going market rate of about 3.5% (instead of the 10% we were paying). This meant a substantial drop in our monthly payments along with being able to pay the home off much more quickly. By this time, the Mailander House remodel episode had been shown many times both in re-runs and on Netflix, and *Fixer Upper* was a well-respected operation in Waco.

    We found a banker who offered to refinance us at a very attractive rate if Marla would move her clinic's account over to his bank. Marla went back to *her* banker and told him that we had found another bank that wanted to give us a great deal on a refinance loan. That lit a fire! Marla's banker could not work fast enough to give us the same deal: no points or origination fees and a very low interest rate for 15 years. To Mr. Banker who denied us at first but came around after two years, all I can say is: "Oh, ye of little faith!"

Chapter 6   Hijacked by a Film Crew

We had little idea how much our lives were about to change by being on this new show based on the work of a local couple. After investigating the *Fixer Upper* show a bit, I figured that we could only benefit because TV programs have substantial budgets and our house would probably turn out well. However, it was a bit of a gamble for both *Fixer Upper* (would we be duds on camera?) and us (would the house be in good condition after the work?). As the old saying goes, "Nothing ventured, nothing gained."

Marla tells a story:

Chip and Joanna had influence on how the houses were remodeled; they could say 'yes' or 'no' to a house; they had the ability to do all the remodeling and decorating. The TV production company they worked with at that time simply documented the process and created drama (through editing). The only requirement related to filming was that the owner of the house had to complete and pass a Skype interview with someone from the production company. I was assured, off the record, that the interview was just to verify that participants would not clam-up on TV and were not "batshit crazy."

And another story from Gail, who was Marla's driver for the episode:

I was totally clueless about the filming because no one had told me what to expect. Marla and I had three cars to choose from, one was the Ford Escape, and that's what we chose at random. We left the Corvette and the Ford pickup. No one explained that it would be my driving skills, which I have very few of, and my vehicle, that were going to feature in the show. If I had known that, we would have brought the Corvette!

The film producer, Corina, said that would never work because she planned on hiding in the back seat. She crouched down in the back seat and told us to start driving. Pick a route and just go somewhere, and talk about something--start a conversation between us in the front seat. She said that we should talk about neighborhoods and houses we were driving by.

When we got to the bumpy road around where the old Parkview Christian School was, Corina said (from the backseat), 'Find a smoother road.' And through all of this, the Waco policeman assigned to the filming continued to follow us. When I used my turn signal because the policeman was behind me, Corina said 'Don't do that, it will mess up the sound. When you talk, that click click click of the signal is audible.' And I didn't say, 'Well there's a policeman behind us,' because I knew she could not see him because she was hiding in the back seat. Since I couldn't use a turn signal, I was constantly checking my rearview mirror.

We drove to each of the houses that we were supposedly considering buying. And we know that story [inferring that the actual home was already selected before the filming]. *The way the show works is buyers have already purchased something* [which will be remodeled by Magnolia]. *That's the staged part of it.*

When we arrived at each location, I was pretty much toured through the house and somebody pointed to part of the house and said, 'So you say something.' [Marla adds that nobody was scripted]. *They gave me the opportunity to comment on the kitchen in one of them. It didn't have a dishwasher. And I said, 'Well, it needs a dishwasher.' Marla said she could do without a dishwasher, and I was supposed to convince her that she needed a dishwasher. So, I went over there, placed my hands on her shoulders, and said, 'You need a dishwasher,' and I think that's in the show.*

We got to hang out with Chip and Joanna the entire time, and they're just exactly like they seem on the show. Chip's kind of a wild goofy sort of guy, kind of a daredevil. On TV he is just like he is in person, horsing around all the time. And Joanna is just going, 'Chip, Chip, down, down.' She's focusing on the decorating and looking at how she is going to move a wall. She's trying to settle him down and she's looking at where she can remove the wall, put in the recessed lighting, the farmhouse door and sink, and oh, poured concrete countertops. No problem. They look at the potential to use things Joanna has designed or that go with her decorator taste. I think she looks at it and says, 'I can really turn this into a showplace."

In actuality, of course, there is no way that *Fixer Upper* can start work on a house their clients don't own yet, so there is a bit of artifice in the "reality." Marla and I were ready to buy the house with our own money, but with the Loan Fish in the picture, all the financing wound up becoming a mixed-bag because the Loan Fish would now hold title to the property until we paid him back $65,000. It was not bad for us personally, and it worked well for both the TV show and the lender, but it increased the pressure on us to get things done quickly, such as providing photographs of Marla and I together, completing many back-story questionnaires, and signing a multitude of documents online and via fax. Marla and I both held full-time jobs, so this was a bit much, but we knew it was a one-time opportunity, so we went for it. Where there is risk, there is also an opportunity for great success. And I'm OK with failure, too, if no one gets an eye put out!

After Marla and Gail did the house tours and Marla "chose" the Mailander House, the camera crew filmed a segment where Marla visits Chip and Joanne's ranch to look at concrete kitchen countertops. I suggested concrete countertops, as they are less pretentious than granite or marble and fit the rustic cottage style of the house. Concrete is about the same price as granite, but less swank. In 20 years, someone will not want to tear it out – it gathers beauty with age. As part of the filming, Marla also played their veterinarian (complete with black bag) and gave immunization shots to two puppies that Chip had just procured. It's an endearing part of the episode, showing the Gaines's little kids playing with the puppies – unscripted and preciously cute. (Chip subsequently procured two more puppies and one of his assistants has brought them to Marla's clinic for immunization. It is fun for us to be their doggy doctor!)

Prior to filming, Marla and Gail had never seen *Fixer Upper* and had no knowledge of how the show worked. According to Marla, *"I thought it was like* This Old House - *an old houses story. I found an old house. They remodeled it. This is what it costs. This is what we do. I had no idea that entertainment would be part of the process. In retrospect it was probably good that we had not seen other episodes*

- we just winged it without advance preparation. I don't believe they wanted it to be anything other than natural on our part. The dramatic characters were Chip and Chip. When we finally decided to watch one show, it was the one with the rat. Eating the roach [by Chip] had not happened yet. It was the very first one, where the lady of the house was shocked by the giant dead rat in the kitchen.*

Gail adds some details to the story:

So, one day, I think it was Sunday when the workmen were not there, Marla and I stopped by Mailander House during one of our training runs. We were on the side of the house and found a large black desiccated cat. The cat had probably died under the house and some workmen put it on the ground over by the trash cans, probably to be thrown away later. The trash cans were already full. The dead cat at Mailander was going to be a problem. I don't know why I felt that way, but I thought it was going to be a problem in the episode.

So, we decided to bury the cat properly. I went and bought a nice big rosemary bush - the kind that live in many yards. And there was a circle of stones in the yard with some herbs growing there, so we decided to bury it there, in that circle. We called that cat 'Rosemary' because that plant is taking up nutrients from the bones of that cat. Rosemary the Cat, that's what his name is.

During filming, Marla also visited Joanna at the Magnolia offices on Bosque Street to see the computer simulation of how *Fixer Upper* would remodel the interior of our house. All in, this filming took about a week of Marla's time, during which her clinic was without its primary doctor! Marla was able to fill-in with relief veterinarians, but this, of course, costs money instead of making it. Marla was having fun but worried about bleeding red at her clinic. At the time, we wondered if all this filming was going to work out — would the house turn out well, or had we made a very expensive mistake? Wonder, yes; give up, NO!

Marla relates:

To enter a <u>Fixer Upper</u> arrangement, at least at that time [First Season in 2014], there were a couple of things we had to be ready to do. We had to be ready to give over control - to give an artistic license. The finances and those sorts of things were clear - we could control how our money was being spent because we had an agreed-upon budget with Magnolia. It was clear that the most esthetic benefit would come from following the 'spirit of the show' - the idea that Chip and Joanna found a house for us and fixed it up to make us happy.

To me, because that was the show, that was real, adopting that state of mind had the best potential for the most gain. The real advantage to having a Fixer Upper remodel, instead of doing it ourselves, was the design work that Chip and Joanna would do when given free rein. Without free rein, if an owner went in and started making suggestions, nothing would have been accomplished very quickly [in our case it was very quick - just one month]. I simply said, 'These things are what I must have,' and with everything else, I must let Chip and Joanna do their magic. I had a list of what I 'must have' [roof that does not leak, toilets that flush, etc.] and we agreed to a budget for the house and work they had to accomplish.

Our simple budget agreement made it clear that the plantings in the front yard, flagstones near the porch, the light fixtures, those were things the Fixer Upper show provided us and did not charge us for. I selected the color of the stone kitchen floor and said that I wanted the house to still look old when they were done. In terms of little things, like where the light fixtures went [recessed ceiling lights], I did not exert a lot of control. But as I think about it, look back on it, mostly because the house didn't undergo a lot of change, it was not a huge remodel. They took out a wall, put in a farmhouse sink, installed recessed lighting, built a kitchen island, and decorated in a style that I was likely to find inspirational.

That was the theme, and it was a very simple arrangement. It was the most uncomplicated 30 days of a house being taken from 'left for dead' to a house that ultimately was pleasant to live in. It might not be the best house in the world; after all, it is 108 years old, has tiny closets, a microscopic bathroom in the front, and a larger bathroom in the back with no shower. We changed very little of the footprint of the house, partly due to economics, but partly because it's such a neat house overall with its open floor plan.

Chapter 7   The Reveal

As work started to progress quickly on Mailander House, the Magnolia/*Fixer Upper* team strictly prohibited us from driving by, being on the property, or asking others to check on it and report back to us. They wanted The Reveal (when owners see their remodeled home for the first time) to be an honest first look by us. This was easy for me as I was 1,600 miles away in San Luis Obispo teaching! But at least once a day, the film crew kept seeing a silver Subaru wagon driving by the house. This elicited several frantic calls from the assistant producer to Marla's business manager for Marla to stop driving by the house while it was being remodeled! Truth be told, there was a Baylor law school student who lived about three houses away, around the corner on 4th St. And guess what she drove? Her car was not identical to Marla's, but it was a silver Subaru wagon. The neighbor had the non-turbo charged version called the Impreza - it lacked the hood scoop that our WRX model has. We were amused by the ignorance of "Subarudom" by these production assistants!

After only three weeks remodeling and filming, the time came for 'The Husband' (me) to make my appearance. A main premise of our episode is Chip saying, "Marla's husband is coming to Waco and we have to get the house ready for him." That was completely true, but we did not know when the house remodel would be ready for us to see. It had been a rainy spring which delayed some of the painting and roofing work, but there was a production schedule to keep!

On short notice, the production company bought me a ticket to fly from California to Waco for a shoot. At the time, my class schedule was open on Wednesday only. We had one day to get my segment of the shooting done. I caught a late flight out to Texas on Tuesday evening, arriving in Waco on the last puddle-jumper from Dallas. It was a bittersweet visit with my new wife Marla, less than 24 hours, but I was still glad for it. Chalk up a bonus point for the TV show that I could spend a day with my wife and someone else paid for the airline ticket!

As Marla recalls:

Part of the anxiety was that The Reveal is a REALLY big day. Even then, the first season, Reveals attracted crowds. If anyone knew there was a Reveal, they would find a parking space to watch. We had very little time to figure out what we were going to do, because Dave was teaching at college in California, and he didn't have the ability to be here for more than a day. The Reveal date was not decided upon in time for him to stay more than one day or for him to even get a cheap plane ticket.

In fact, the show had to cover the cost of the plane ticket on short notice because Dave had already come a week or so before for the original Reveal date, but it turned out that Chip and Joanna were on a trip somewhere. So, we were working around a production schedule that was developing spontaneously as it went. Dave had gotten off the plane from California around 11 p.m. and was going to film The Reveal the next day, then get back on the plane at five p.m. He was in Waco for less than one day.

Just a note about The Reveal; this is a funny story I remember. Once it became known that 'my veterinarian [Marla] *is on TV', I had a lot of clients coming in just to talk about the show. The most common question was, 'Did you get to keep the furniture?' Well, there could be a whole chapter on that question as I was asked it so many times! No, we didn't get to keep the furniture, but we were able to purchase it at an affordable price if we wanted to. If it is something that Joanna had purchased at the market, she sells it to the client at her cost. We kept the coffee table, some light fixtures, the ladder* [used as a towel rack in the bathroom] *and other things that she had bought at market. Some of the decorator items had come from Marshalls. Before Joanna had Magnolia Market, she was a very shrewd shopper. Joanna could find things that look great wherever she needed them for a job, so that was kind of fun.*

But back to The Reveal story. Two years after our show, The Reveals were becoming events not to be missed if one lived in Waco. When I told one of my clients that we were going to be renting our fixer-upper on Vacation Rental By Owner or Airbnb, she said, "Good. Maybe I can send my grandchildren over there. They love <u>Fixer Upper</u> and honestly if I could just get them out of the house that would be great."

She added, "When there was a <u>Fixer Upper</u> being worked on just up the block from us, my nine-year-old granddaughter wanted to go every day because she wanted to see Chip. I told her, 'Well, you know you can't bother him; he's working, and they won't be able to stop what they're doing to talk to you. And she said, 'But Grandma, if he is in the porta potty, can I just go up to the door and knock on it and talk to him when he comes out?'" I said, 'You know, you're right; you've got a precocious little granddaughter.' I told my client that normally we don't let small children in the house because there is a lot of old glass that is low on the walls and doors, but her granddaughter, I thought, would be fine.

During the filming of this segment of our episode, we were to be shown our renovated house (The Reveal), then mount our bicycles and head off to Cameron Park along the Brazos River Trail. The Reveal involves the film crew installing a large billboard-type image of our old house for us to see as we drive up. We could not see the new house behind the giant screen. They made us cover our eyes and walked us toward the house. Then Chip and Joanna ask, "Are you ready to see your Fixer Upper?" We say, "Yes!" Then, they pull the screen away and the remodeled house is revealed to us, the buyers.

Honestly, the house looked damn good. A bunch of nasty old trees were removed, the new roof was on, the paint looked great. Marla and I were honestly impressed by how much they had done in a few weeks. Having done a lot of home remodel physical labor myself, I was very glad the heavy lifting was done! The Magnolia team did a ton of quality work, in short order. I felt delighted that I did not have to remodel this one myself – it's not work for the faint of heart. This type of project is all a calculated risk, and it may sound corny, but Magnolia had our backs.

For this segment of the shoot, the production company was quite clear that all logos and branding were out. We had to wear clothing that had no names on it, which was not a problem. However, we would be riding our own bicycles and wearing our own helmets, which have brand names on them. The gaffers put tape over any words on the bicycles' frames, wheels, and forks and covered the logos on our helmets. The whole effort is to prevent free advertising for a company that does not have a sponsorship agreement with the TV network. It was odd to have black tape all over our bikes and helmets. Editors adjust the taped objects during post-production so that everything looks normal – the audience doesn't see the tape. This is one of those small miracles of modern digital technology.

Waco was very rainy during the spring of 2014, but for this one day of shooting we lucked out and had nice sunny weather; it had been raining through much of the renovation of the house and the film crew was happy for us. Remembering the multiple takes from the commercials I had worked on (in Southern California it is easy to work for the studios), I was ready for the retakes. And there were a lot of them. We were excited during our initial viewing of the home and entry into our Fixer Upper. Doing it a second and third time was kind of fun, although not much of a surprise. The crew kept asking for another retake on The Reveal and initial entry into the home, and it never was boring or flat for me – this type of filming is what I expected.

Marla, however, grew a little weary of the repetition, but we persisted and did about a half-dozen takes of each step in the scene, and toward the end, I will confess we were feigning excitement and surprise. It was not hard for me to smile since I was delighted by how well the house had turned out and that someone else had done all the painting. (I like carpentry, but painting is not my forté.)

I had grown up in Southern California, and in addition to some experience working on commercials, my family had also been on *Family Feud*, so I had some sense of how much time the filming process could take. Marla, being from a very small town in Arkansas, had never been around movie or TV production. She had no idea of the time commitment required to shoot even a small segment of a one-hour TV show (which is only 44 minutes on Cable TV – the rest being commercials). But she learned quickly how many hours of filming are required when the production team took control of her agenda for a week or so. Our *Fixer Upper* episode features Marla and her sister Gail driving around Waco, meeting Chip and Joanna at prearranged houses, and walking through them. The typical *Fixer Upper* program has the married couple seeing the houses - Gail was my stand-in as I was in the middle of a class term and could not leave my teaching job.

Universities typically don't have substitute teachers, and I was committed to my students. I could not, in good conscience, take off a week for filming. The show's formula has the buyer look at three houses and ultimately settle on one that they like, and filming this segment takes many hours. The plot line for our show was that Marla was in a hurry to find a good house because her husband was coming to Waco soon, and she wanted to have a nice home waiting for him. This was true enough. We did need a place to settle in together, and I give all praise and thanks to Team Gaines and crew for getting our newlywed home ready.

When TV producers work in a studio setting, they have a lot of control. Therefore, the industry spends hundreds of millions building and maintaining studios and sets. When a film is shot 'on location' (outside of a film studio) all kinds of things can go wrong, starting with the weather, and there is a lot of pressure to work long hours on favorable days. During the two days Marla and her sister drove around and looked at three houses, the filming took approximately 20 hours. The filming did not stop for lunch; there was hardly a chance to answer the call of nature (one time they used the bathroom at the home of one of the *Fixer Upper* workers, Shorty, for a quick nature break). All this filming work boiled down to maybe 7 or 8 minutes of the TV program that aired. The times that Marla went out to the Gaines' ranch and to the Magnolia office were not so time-consuming or stressful because she did not perform multiple takes.

Chapter 8   Bicycle House

Although it took us five decades to find each other, Marla and I are kindred spirits--we both have an independent streak, a risk-taking quest for adventure, and a desire to embrace the new and unknown. These are beneficial characteristics in tackling the renovation of an old house without a lot of time or money. So, in marrying, I expressed my belief that the causes and conditions that brought us together were ready to blossom. And our life experience gave us focus that helped us say "Yes," when bankers and other stodgy types lacking imagination said, "No."

Independently, Marla and I each found that a willingness to take risks came partly from our having been given bicycles at a young age and then allowed and encouraged to explore and experience the world on them. A bicycle is one of the simplest and most efficient ways to travel and explore, perfect for a child who would grow to be an intrepid traveler. Or, perfect for someone who falls, gets back up, and tries again, a bit wiser but still willing. (See Appendix III for some bicycle history.)

When Chip and Joanna were working on our Fixer Upper house, Joanna wanted to do something extraordinary for me. Although she had never met me, she knew that Marla and I were newlyweds, and she thought it would be fun to make the house super-special for me. When she learned that I was a broken-down old bike racer who still loved riding, albeit more slowly, she was intrigued. When she learned that I love older bikes and the stories of the craftsmen who made them, she knew what to do. She found me an amazing bike to welcome me to our new home. And many of the folks who have seen our episode on *Fixer Upper* remember that cool old bike, too.

I got my first bicycle as a six-year-old, when my family lived in Highland Heights, a small suburb of Cleveland, Ohio. It was a red single speed large-tired bike that my dad bought secondhand for $10. Solid as a Russian tank, it was my escape vehicle from the chaotic maelstrom of life with many younger brothers and sisters. Highland Heights was transitioning from farms into single-family homes, a slow suburbanization. Our street, Franklin Boulevard, was a dirt/gravel road. 'Boulevard' was someone's imagination gone wild!

My backyard neighbor, David Serkey, had a black single speed Schwinn bicycle and a big black Labrador retriever. Serkey and I roamed the neighborhood's dirt roads and adjoining forests on our bikes, with Blackie the Labrador leading the way. Blackie quickly deduced that when the bikes came out, we were headed out for fun in the woods. Serkey would put the hand strap of the dog leash on his handlebars and Blackie would pull like mad down the road heading for our local pond. Blackie would run and play in the woods for hours until we were ready to head back home.

How I loved that simple red bicycle! It was my exploration range-extender, as I could go a lot farther on the bike than I could by walking. What a life! Serkey, Blackie, and I would spend entire summer days out in the woods, catching turtles and frogs, swimming in ponds, and getting a good tan. My mom was a bit worried when I would disappear for hours, but my dad insisted that we be allowed to roam.

Marla grew up in an area of south-central Arkansas where logging is a primary occupation. Her grandfather sharpened saws and ran a logging camp, and the county was criss-crossed by sandy, unpaved logging roads. She and her older sisters loved to roam the woods near their home, exploring creeks and ponds. They, too, used bicycles as range-extenders, venturing to explore a lot farther from home than they could on foot. Marla and her sisters, along with friends, always traveled in clumps of kids, and they took care of one another so the moms rarely worried.

By the time Marla and I met, we had both participated in multiple triathlon events, had upgraded our bicycles considerably, and were still avid cyclists (though I had given up on triathlons due to the running). So, when it came time to decorate our Fixer Upper house, the bicycle was a natural. Waco has been kind to us, and we try to get out on our bikes often, but the 1905 bicycle from Jojo tops the cake as the all-time beauty. When Jojo had the original idea to surprise me with an antique bike as décor for my office, Marla was enthusiastic about the idea, but we were on a budget. Overruns during the *Fixer Upper* remodel had started to hurt a bit – a few thousand here, a few thousand there – ouch! Marla thought she and Jojo could find a nice antique bike for a hundred dollars or so. That might have been the case at one time, but the market has changed--old bikes are cool and desirable, which is reflected in their prices. It didn't help that many old bicycles had been melted down for steel during World War II, limiting available options.

Of course, Marla and Jojo decided eBay was the best option for locating a vintage bike. After losing out on several bikes because Marla did not think they were worth the asking price (but someone else did), Marla and Jojo found me a 1905 Velvet Road Racer bicycle for my office, which cost about six times the original budget estimate. It has wooden rims, rust, and some broken spokes, but the pedals and wheels still turn. It has the original leather saddle and hand grips. It is not ridable but could be restored with love and perseverance. It is the most amazing bike ever, a connection to a time when there were no motor vehicles and life's pace was that of a horse-drawn wagon or human-propelled wheels.

Honeymoon in Zion

Wedding Chapel

Mailander House Before

Mailander House After

Living Room Before

Living Room After

Kitchen Before

Kitchen After

The Reveal

With Chip and Joanna Gaines

Part III Living in a Fixer Upper

Chapter 9 Settling In

"The houses of early Texans were small, but their hearts were large enough to cover all deficiencies. No candidate for hospitality was ever turned away." [1]- Noah Smithwick, on traveling through Texas in the early days.

While it is true that we bought the Mailander House to be close to Cameron Park, a subtler under-current was that Marla needed a fresh start with her new man. She owns, and used to live in, another old house a few miles west of Mailander House. That house, Hound Haven, was built in 1930 by a cotton trader named Gaines deGraffenreid. The deGraffenreids are descended from minor Swiss royalty and Gaines built the house of stone (a small 'man castle') for himself. It is on the West Waco Creek in an area that once abutted a Masonic golf course, a nice part of town. Marla had lived a previous life there that she wanted to break free of so she could start over with her new husband. Our Mailander House was a fresh start for both of us.

With my Fresno house (that I had inherited and remodeled) now sold, it was finally time to head east. I had inherited a houseful of stuff from my dad, and accumulated multiple bicycles and other sports-related items. How many pairs of skis does a guy need in the heart of Texas? My stepmom had given me a book entitled *Stuff,* which helped me decide what to keep. I pruned, pared, and made many trips to the Salvation Army. As moving day approached, I put things on the sidewalk and ran 'Free' ads on Craigslist. Gone was the extra furniture. Gone was the gas BBQ. Gone was the big TV that I had bought from Salvation Army. Gone was the paint, lumber, and

---

[1] *The Evolution of a State, or Recollections of Old Texas Days*. Austin: Steck Company, 1935

yard tools along with all the detritus Dad had left behind. My neighbors thought I was nuts when I told them what I was doing, but they watched it all disappear. I think I created some new believers in the power of Craigslist.

First, we had to shuttle our cars out. During our honeymoon in January, we drove the Subaru WRX out to Waco. In Fresno, I still had Marla's Jeep Wrangler, my Jeep Grand Cherokee, and my Dodge Sprinter. Over the spring, I sold my Jeep to my niece for a song, drove Marla's Jeep out to Texas, and finally, after I completed my semester at Cal Poly, I started to move using the Sprinter.

Because it was impossible to find a U-Haul rental at that time, I bought an enclosed cargo trailer. I made two trips to Waco to get it all here; I like to drive and the scenery in the American Southwest is good. It's about 1,600 miles each way and I learned the route well. On the first trip, Marla flew out to drive with me for a while, and I remember watching the fireworks on Independence Day in Yuma, Arizona, where we stayed on our first night. Who would choose Yuma for a holiday celebration? It was the luck of the draw for us, and we just appreciated wherever we found ourselves and made it fun.

The next day we made it to Albuquerque, New Mexico, and I took her to the airport so she could get back to Waco and her clinic; then I pushed on driving by myself. The summer of 2014 was not too hot and only once did the Sprinter start to overheat on a long grade. That was outside Flagstaff, AZ, and I just slowed down and took it easy on the long uphill until the road topped out into flatter areas where the diesel motor did not have to work so hard. I think both the trailer and the Sprinter were maxed out on that trip, so it was no surprise.

After a long day's drive across West Texas, I finally arrived at Mailander House at dusk. I clearly remember Marla laughing at me as I danced around with ants biting my feet. I was walking in sandals through the grass of our new home to our side porch when suddenly my feet were on fire. I started hopping around, and probably looked like a real greenhorn. Fire ants, when disturbed, bite, injecting a venom that burns and causes white pustules to form afterwards. Red and black fire ants are native to South America, but they were accidentally introduced into the U.S. around the 1930s through the port of Mobile, Alabama and have been spreading since. Unbeknownst to me, those suckers were well entrenched in our lawn and they did not appreciate being trod upon by the feet of man.

I found in moving goods from the street to the house that I always had to review my path for 'interesting critters.' Here in Waco I have encountered, in addition to fire ants, copperhead snakes, spiders up to three inches across, and many flying wasps and hornets. Really, the only ones that have caused me serious problems are the ants. As it says in the Bible, *"The meek shall inherit the earth."* Not many things meeker than a ¼ inch long insect, and now I always give those fire ants a wide berth. Heaven forbid I should give my loving wife ammunition to laugh at me again.

As we settled in that first summer in 2014, it took a while to adapt to being in each other's space full time. Marla had decorated Mailander House wonderfully. Then I showed up with my stuff, which didn't exactly match the décor she envisioned. Mailander House was not overflowing with closet space, and my first gift to Marla for our new home was a very tidy large shed for the backyard. We ordered it from a local Mennonite business, and it was delivered on a blustery December day. To Marla's great delight, we had more storage!

Marla and her sister Gail are very close. Marla is the youngest of four girls, and all the older sisters took care of the youngest. Gail, being the closest in age, spent a lot of time with Marla growing up, and we were very happy to move close to them in Waco. Gail's husband Dan is a retired Army colonel and he and I became good friends, having much in common as Eagle Scouts and outdoors enthusiasts. That first summer we all kayaked in the Brazos River, attended running races where the girls competed in 50-mile or longer races, and shared many BBQs and parties. Waco quickly felt like home.

Once our episode aired on TV, we had quite a few unexpected visitors. Some delightful folks stopped by unexpectedly on a Sunday afternoon as we were hanging out at the house after lunch. I was used to people slowing down to have a look at the house, but they never came up to the door and asked to chat with us. However, on that afternoon, a nicely dressed older couple (obviously coming from church) got out and walked up to the door. The gentleman was wearing a suit, and his wife was wearing a very nice dress, lovely shoes, and a big beautiful hat. When they knocked on the door, I went to answer.

I was a little suspicious because folks who want to proselytize get on my nerves, and these folks were dressed like the ones who hand out those little inspirational pamphlets. However, I opened the door and the visitors introduced themselves rather formally. I said my name and called Marla to the door. We introduced ourselves, and they said they had seen us on the television show. I thought, what the heck, let's invite them in. They came in and we all sat down in the living room. Marla went to make tea, which left me with the burden of being polite and making conversation with new acquaintances. I asked them where they came from, how they liked the show, and what they were doing that afternoon. Of course, people love to talk about themselves; all we have to do is give them a chance and show interest.

The gentleman explained that his wife was a big fan of *Fixer Upper* and she loved our house. They were coming from a church service at the Mount Zion Missionary Baptist Church. We asked them where they lived and what their house was like. They said they lived in Bellmead, a town about six miles east. They reported their house was nothing fancy, but they really liked it and took care of it. They then praised our house for what a wonderful job had been done by the Magnolia people and said they really liked the way we were keeping up the yard, planting new flowers, and beautifying the home.

After a few more minutes of pleasantries, they took their leave, inviting us to visit them. The man went to great lengths to explain where their house was and how we could find it when we came to visit. I think everyone knew that we wouldn't really come to visit, but they felt it was important to make the offer. And we certainly appreciated their manners and politeness. After their visit, we realized that what they really wanted was to see if the house was as beautiful as it appeared on television. This was the first of many visits from strangers (all polite and well-mannered). Their goal was to see for themselves if reality TV is a hoax or the real deal.

Chapter 10   Plumbing Hell

Dante's 14th century *Divine Comedy* described nine levels of *inferno* (Hell in Italian). My personal Hell was probably more of a purgatory--that period of suffering that expiates sin and brings redemption. Plumbing has a long history of improving human life. One of the first things developing nations do is promote clean water and proper disposal and treatment of waste. In the US, we spend billions of public dollars annually maintaining our infrastructure due to all those pipes underground. Or, as in our case at Mailander House, the pipes were underground in our yard, under our house, and in our walls. We were personally responsible for any repairs. We feel proud that over the past few years we helped contribute substantial amounts of cash in the effort to improve American domestic infrastructure - and local contractors have the new trucks (with our money) to prove it! We spent considerable money and time in our quest for redemption during our time in purgatory.

Our initial contract with Magnolia and *Fixer Upper* included five thousand dollars for "plumbing upgrades." I have made a note to myself that, in the future, exactly what work will be performed in an upgrade will be spelled out in detail. In our case, Magnolia fixed all glaring problems by repairing and replacing as needed. The kitchen plumbing was replaced along with the water supply line from the street. Additional repairs were restricted to the house only. In our first few months living at Mailander House, we noticed that the shower drained slowly, and occasionally a toilet backed up. We just figured that this is how old houses go, and initially we spent money on things like a new garage door and backyard fencing for our pooch.

By autumn we had some extra money; I had sold my house in California and Marla had gained many new clients at her clinic from what we called the 'Magnolia Effect.' People who had seen Marla on TV brought their pets in just to visit with a real 'star.' Marla's TV career was more like a small meteorite than a star, but we were glad for the increased business. She was a star to those clients, and we took that money she earned and gave it to our plumbers. We took on the issue of the shower not draining well in a big way and wound up hiring plumbers to repair and replace a lot of the wastelines under the house that *Magnolia* had not worked on. After several expensive work sessions, the plumbers got the wastelines under the house in good shape and functioning as expected.

We had some dramatic rain in Waco during 2014, the first year I lived here. In Central Texas, rainstorms seem to come from the south, the west and the north. Seattle has about the same annual rainfall as Waco, but in contrast to Seattle's frequent light drizzle, Waco rains are often quite violent, dropping large volumes of water in short order. Central Texas seems to be a meeting ground of warm moist air from the south (Gulf of Mexico) and cooler air, usually from the north. When the two meet, the cooler air slides under the warmer air and cools it, which can cause rapid condensation. Once the warm, moist air cools sufficiently, dramatic rainfall and sometimes tornadoes result. It is not uncommon for streets in low-lying areas of Waco to flood a foot or more for a few hours during a storm. Then there are sometimes periods of many weeks without any rain and the soil becomes very dry.

That first summer while cutting the grass, I noticed some uneven ground in one part of the backyard. Some areas grew grass more heavily than others. Again, I attributed this to an old house. As the fall and winter rains came on, I noticed some ground in the backyard was almost marshy, and a pronounced 'swamp gas' smell was prevalent. I first suspected that the wasteline, extending about 100 feet to the alley behind the house, was clogged with tree roots and was perhaps leaking as well. Our plumber came and ran an electric snake through the line to break up and flush roots. Then he ran a camera through the line to look for breaks. We were not happy with what he found.

Much of the waste line to the alley was very old clay pipe. In a few places, plastic pipe had been spliced in to replace broken clay pipe. New breaks had appeared, and when the soil was saturated by heavy rain, waste water leaked out and spread just below the surface. This had been happening in summer, too – which explained the super happy grass in some parts of the yard. With the winter marsh effect, we knew something had to be done soon.

Our intrepid plumber, never one to turn down an honest dollar, agreed to replace the line in the middle of February 2015. Like the previous year, 2015 was a very wet winter. First, he mapped the existing line and excavated a new trench around it. He had a dandy little tractor-trencher machine that did most of the heavy digging. Once they got near the line, the manual shovel work began. Mailander House is built on a heavy clay soil called "Blackland Prairie." This soil is never easy to dig in the best of conditions, but in winter digging becomes a heavy sticky mess. The plumbers certainly earned their keep digging the required long trench. We were smart enough to negotiate a set price for the work and not pay by the hour.

Unfortunately for the plumbers, they dug a nice clean ditch on Friday, and then decided to come back and finish the work after a three-day weekend. Of course, it rained like mad over the holiday weekend. The trench became a moat, and some dirt slid in, creating a heavy goo and burying the pipe at the bottom. When the plumbers returned on Tuesday, it was like a scene out of the Battle of Verdun. The trench had to be pumped out and then the heavy mud re-dug. To compound the battle, there was often a light rain to increase the diggers' misery – they were wet above and in cold mud below. The plumbers worked fast and replaced the entire line in one push. They did a partial refill of the trench to keep the pipe in one place and waited for drier weather. We did get a reprieve from the rain for a week, so the tractor came back and leveled the ground. The swamp gas smell and marsh condition went away, at least for a while.

One of the characteristics of Blackland Prairie soil is that it expands when saturated with water. Likewise, when it dries, it shrinks and can form deep cracks. While it is a superb soil for agriculture, it presents problems for light building foundations. This can also affect plumbing, especially plastic pipe with glued joints. Our 2015 summer was one of heavy rains followed by some weeks of punishing heat without rain. The soil responds to the changing moisture by swelling and shrinking. Our new wasteline, which had been installed in rainy conditions, was one of the casualties. Fortunately, it was just a flesh wound, albeit a bit stinky, and the plumbers completed a repair in half a day.

As a note to those considering plumbing work in their own home, the glue joint on plastic pipe must be clean and dry. It is likely that the line installed in February had a joint that did not bond properly because water had contaminated the area to be glued; it was raining the whole time they were working. Fortunately, this repair to the original work did the trick, and we did not have to pay further.

During this time, Marla and I morphed from the initial excitement of our new house, slowly assuming a stoic demeanor interspersed with periods of mild anxiety about what was next. Our neighbors were very happy that we had made the old house look sharp, but they must have also been amused by the monthly stream of contractor trucks at the house. We wanted to know when the expenses would end! I initially looked at the wasteline as a modest engineering project, coupled with a sleuth hunt. From the initial signs of a leak right through the big dig, I was excited to get things fixed and move on to the next project. My only regret is that we did not tackle the digging earlier so we could have avoided the large winter moat though the back lawn.

Mailander House has a small basement with concrete walls and floor. An electric sump pump pushes water out of the basement if it collects. The basement doesn't flood, but because of cracks in the concrete walls, water seeps in from the outside when there are heavy winter rains. The cracks could not be permanently sealed due to the expansive clay soil, so I did the next best thing —drain as much water as possible away from the house during heavy rains.

The engineering solution was obvious. Happily, I was able to accomplish the task with no digging. I observed the rain under storm conditions and provided a simple prescription: gutters and flex hoses to pipe the roof runoff out into the yard well away from the house. Because Mailander had a partial installation of vintage half circle metal gutters, I could not just go to the hardware store to duplicate them. I found a local specialty company, and they came out and installed matching gutters where they were missing.

On my out-building, which was an old carriage house that we had transformed into a bike workshop, I installed gutters bought from a hardware store. They did not have the high-quality of the custom gutters, but they worked OK and I could do them myself. On all the main downspouts of each building, I attached large corrugated flex pipe to move water away from the building. Over the next few years, this made a big difference in keeping both buildings dry. While it is a fuss to keep the gutters clean as we have many trees in the yard, I am philosophical. As the Buddhists say, "Before enlightenment, chop wood and carry water. After enlightenment, chop wood and carry water." There is no escaping keeping gutters clean to have them work correctly.

Fast forward to late 2016, and our Mailander House was rented on Airbnb and VRBO. We had numerous guest groups each week, and one lucky Friday morning one of my guests called. "Dave, we were on the front porch sipping coffee and we smelled natural gas. What should we do?" Happily, the firemen at the station across the street were not on a call and were glad to come over and chat with our attractive female guests.

I jumped in my car and got there about ten minutes after the guests called me. When I arrived, there was a big hook-and-ladder truck out front of Mailander and seven firemen, plus my two guests, assembled on and around the porch. The big rig was called because that unit carried a gas detector –they were looking for methane (the main constituent of domestic natural gas). Sure enough, the detector found flammable gas under the porch and the firemen turned off my gas meter. What now?

While the guests went to breakfast, I waited for the gas company technician who had been called by the firemen. The technician used a gas detector probe to look for methane under the soil in the front lawn where the gas line was presumably buried. He found nothing, and determined the leak was on the house side of the gas meter. Of course, he disconnected the gas meter completely and locked it out. This meant several things. In the short-term, there would be no hot water or gas to cook with. I had to find a place for my guests to stay while repairs were undertaken. The ladies were gracious and understanding, and we put them up in the best hotel in town. I also promised them a free stay if they wanted to come back another time.

Because the city had been notified of the gas leak by the utility company, I had to hire a licensed plumber to complete the repair. I later discovered that the repair could have been a very simple thing, but it cost us about two thousand dollars to figure it out. The plumbers wound up replacing the entire old iron gas line with modern flex line, from the meter on the side of the house to the water heater, dryer, and kitchen stove. It took them several days and numerous trips to their shop and the specialty plumbing supply store. The problem turned out to be a no-brainer; it was just a small end cap that was perforated. I could have fixed it myself in short order. However, the city requires a licensed plumber if the plumbing issue involves flammable gas. We had no choice, so we just sighed and shook our heads.

In the early days of domestic natural gas supply, there was potential for dirt and grit to get into the pipes. Consequently, plumbers installed a sediment trap into the supply line – essentially a short pipe a few inches long teed into the supply line facing downward. Grit will drop into this short pipe and collect, protecting the appliances downstream from clogging. In the old days, natural gas also contained some water vapor and sulfur compounds that might also collect in the sediment trap.

We have no idea how old the gas line supplying Mailander was, but the sediment trap probably collected its share of water vapor and sulfurous gas. When sulfur in the gas-phase mixes with water, it creates sulfuric acid. Over time, this accumulation of acid probably ate a hole in the metal cap at the end of the sediment trap, allowing gas to leak out. If we had proactively replaced the small leaking cap of the sediment trap, it would have cost less than a latte at the local coffee shop. Having the foresight to inspect and replace little things could save a lot of money in the long run.

Again, we were fortunate that our plumbers could fix the problem for us quickly. On the day it was completed, I stayed in the house to wait for the city inspector to sign off on the work so the gas company could restore our service. I spent almost twelve hours at the house waiting for the inspection. The City of Waco inspector apparently came in the early afternoon, but never knocked on the door or called me on my cell number to let me know we were good to go. In a state of semi-panic, I called the city office at 4:50 p.m. asking when the inspection was going to happen. The dispatcher checked and informed me that the new gas line had been approved hours before. I was peeved at the apparent lack of competence and communication in the inspection process. The inspector did not even go under the house to see the new line, because that required a key, which I had. If he is not going to "inspect," then what am I paying for? It's little things like this that make some people say that government is broken.

Thankfully, our natural gas company has around-the-clock technicians who will reconnect meters and restore service. After talking to the city, I was able to schedule a gas company service tech that evening. He did not arrive for some hours, but by ten that night the gas was back on and everything was working normally. Marla took pity on me and brought me a nice dinner during my time of incarceration at Mailander waiting for the service technician.

When all was said and done, during our first year at Mailander, we spent about $20,000 on upgrades and repairs beyond what Magnolia had done. This work included a new garage door, backyard fence with gates, storm doors, and plumbing. Fortunately, we knew going in that we were buying an old house and that Magnolia was working within our meager budget. If we had had a better banker, we may have been able to complete more repair work before we moved in. C'est la vie.

Chapter 11   The Wise Man Built His House Upon the Rock

In the King James Version of the Bible's book of Matthew, it is written:

> 7:24 Therefore whosoever heareth these sayings of mine, and doeth them, I will liken him unto a wise man, which built his house upon a rock: 25 and the rain descended, and the floods came, and the winds blew, and beat upon that house; and it fell not: for it was founded upon a rock. 26 And every one that heareth these sayings of mine, and doeth them not, shall be likened unto a foolish man, which built his house upon the sand: 27 and the rain descended, and the floods came, and the winds blew, and beat upon that house; and it fell: and great was the fall of it.

There is much wisdom there, although it seems that places like Houston forgot their Bible study when they decided where they should build (the part about the rains descending and the floods). In 1969, as a lad in Southern California, I saw an entire new subdivision near our home heavily damaged by relentless rain and poor drainage engineering. The developer lost so much money he committed suicide. Seeing this carnage at age 14 helped me realize that poor land use decisions, poor engineering, and ignorance of weather patterns can mean disaster. Conversely, good decisions can avert all kinds of trouble. As a kid, I was amazed by some of the choices adults made, but now I realize that choices are often based on short-term profit rather than long-term sustainability.

During our association with *Fixer Upper*, they did all the grunt work, including the foundation work. The irony was that our lowball budget came back to haunt us. Chip had estimated $1,500 to "level the house." What that meant was that the Magnolia building team lifted the corner near the back bathroom and poured a new concrete stem wall underneath to support it. When the cement cured, they lowered the house back down and tied the plumbing back in. At least that is what I assume they did. I was teaching in San Luis Obispo at the time so could not really observe all the magic. And Marla was under strict orders from Joanna and the TV producers NOT to visit the house while work was going forward; they did not want to spoil the surprise at The Reveal.

After the filming was done, Marla had to wait a couple of weeks to move in. A team that had only three weeks to fix up a house left for dead could not possibly have the house move-in ready. The Magnolia team completed all the cosmetics (like drywalling and painting) in the front part of the house, and then tied in plumbing and wiring after the filming was done. Many people experienced with home remodeling have asked us how Magnolia finished the house in just three weeks. Our answer is, "They didn't." It took several more weeks to knock out work in the rest of the house to make it livable.

However, we did not expect to see the cracks appearing in the walls of every room just a few months after we moved in. The arches on either side of the living room fireplace had cracks wide enough to insert a man's finger. This was not auspicious. We had paid Magnolia $65K, and I thought they owed us a house that showed well and did not have cracks throughout, so we called the project manager for our construction. Lindsay came over right away, walked through the house with us, and took pictures. I was very happy to hear her say, "I better call Chip; he needs to come over."

In a flurry of phone calls between Magnolia and Marla's office manager, Dotti, a pow-wow was set up to look at the house and negotiate. The meeting was set for an afternoon at Mailander House. Dotti, being a smart southern woman, appeared early with fresh-baked cookies to set up tea and coffee service. At the appointed time, Chip arrived with Lindsay and a structural engineer. For the Mailander team, we had Marla, Dotti, and me. Dotti led off with small talk, enjoying pleasantries and a bit to eat and drink. We chatted and made polite conversation for about ten minutes.

While I recognized that this introductory period is both civilized and beneficial to the outcome, I was chomping at the bit to get started. For once, I was able to keep my big mouth shut and smile politely, allowing others to discuss the health of Chip's new puppies and how his kids were doing in softball. All praise and thanks to Dotti for understanding how to conduct a meeting. If it starts off on the right foot, there is a better chance of a positive outcome for everyone.

Once we started discussing the cracks and foundation problems, we toured the house. Chip and his team noted every crack and problem. Then, we sat back down at the table for a little discussion. The structural engineer explained that the soil upon which Mailander was built is expansive clay. I had figured this out already by observation. My background in civil engineering meant that I had seen plenty of building damage in California from expansive soils, and could sling the jargon with the best of them. However, I resisted interrupting and let him speak his piece, as other folks at the table might need to hear it.

The structural engineer explained that modern houses are often built on concrete slabs designed for expansive soils. Mailander House was built using a pier and beam system common at the time. Unfortunately, in areas with expansive soils, pier and beam systems often allow the house to shift— no one argued about this. The engineer suggested that to correct the problem, it might be necessary to drill numerous 16-foot deep bores under the house to reach bedrock, and then fill these with steel and concrete to support the house. He did not know that I had worked on such a project when I was at the University of California Santa Barbara. In that case, the homeowner was quite wealthy and did not want his house to slide down the canyon in the backyard. Considering Santa Barbara real estate values, especially for a house with an ocean view, the money he spent on 16-foot deep borings was a good investment. In Waco, one should consider other options.

After the engineer finished, there was a pregnant pause. Everyone sat silently, including me. Then Dotti and I pulled out our ace, the contract stating that Magnolia would "level the house" for $1,500. I got out a bubble level and demonstrated that in no way were the floors level, and more-over, the house was shifting and causing cracked walls in all the rooms. Chip looked at the level on the floor. He looked at the contract. He looked at the cracked walls. He scratched his head and thought for little bit. Then he stated, "We said we would level the house, and I guess we better take care of it." God bless Chip; one must respect his business acumen.

Chip may have funky hairstyles, but he is nobody's fool. First, Chip said that he would do something, and he honestly believes his word is his bond; if it isn't right, he will make it right. Second, Chip probably realized that a lawsuit or nasty publicity about shoddy workmanship would endanger both his TV show contract and possibly the Magnolia brand. By working to remedy our problem quietly and quickly, he was both following his own moral compass and protecting the business that he and Joanna had worked so hard to build.

Lindsay worked out the details. Magnolia engaged a foundation repair firm that does considerable work on large buildings and expensive homes. The foundation company's bid was not inexpensive, but a deal was cut. Normally, the work on Mailander would have cost about $20K. The contractor agreed to do all the work for half-price with the stipulation that all future foundation work would go to them. Then, Magnolia agreed to pay $5K and we paid $5K. It was a solution that worked for everyone.

When it came time to do the work in late October, I blocked out my entire day. Finally, I would see what was going on and ensure that the work was to my satisfaction. A crew of seven men showed up about sunrise and got busy. They arrived in two trucks pulling large trailers carrying dozens of hydraulic jacks and concrete pillars. The foreman, Jefe, set up a base station in the house to measure floor elevations while the other men deployed the jacks and materials under the house. To a man, the workers were all short, probably averaging about 5'4". This is a real advantage when crawling around under a house all day. The men were all from El Salvador, and I had a good time practicing my Spanish. I'm not sure how much fun they had with me and my poor Spanish grammar, but they were tolerant and amused.

Jefe set the base station in a central doorway between the front sitting room and the dining room. This base station is connected to a long tube that is moved about the house, and the difference in height registers on a digital gauge on the base station. The goal was to level our house to within 1/10" over the entire floor area. Jefe used a radio to talk to the men under the house. Over the course of a long day, Jefe had the men underneath gradually raise the house in strategic areas to bring the whole structure to level with the base station. Then, the men underneath placed concrete piers and steel plates to support the house where it had been raised. Along about dark, the work was finally done; the men pulled out all the jacks and extra piers, loaded up their trucks, and left.

I was intrigued by how this technology worked. How could Jefe determine the elevation all over the house relative to the base station using a simple tube? I did a little research and learned that it is a no-brainer. Using an ancient principle, the modern technology consists of a sensitive digital pressure gauge connected with tubing to a sealed fluid-filled reservoir. The pressure differential between the digital display and reservoir is determined by the height difference and provides accurate, repeatable elevation measurements of + or − level to 1/10". It does not matter how far the measurement point is from the base station in the building, so the contractors were able to reach and level every corner of our house. Of course, this system only works on one floor of a house at a time. Since Mailander House is just one story, it was straightforward work. What a blessing to have the house leveled in one day! A few weeks after all the walls had settled in, Magnolia sent out some workmen who repaired the drywall and repainted. Everything looked just like new and everyone was happy.

So, here we are a few years later. Some small cracks have appeared. I have spent a fair amount of time under the house and have found that the new piers move a bit. I shim the piers with steel plates that the workers left behind, and, over time, I think we may reach a sort of homeostasis. Given the expansive soil we have, I have tried to keep the perimeter of the house hydrated by running soaker hoses around the outside of the foundation. I can't dry the ground in winter, but I can try to keep it damp in summer. It is not a perfect solution, but I'm not trying to make the perfect the enemy of the good. Our goal is to help our good old gal, Mailander House, live another 100 years.

A final note on cracks in the walls. When the Mailanders built the house, they used batten boards and plaster for the walls over a timber frame. The walls then had wallpaper applied. These frame walls covered with semi-elastic paper could move with the foundation as the soil beneath shrank and swelled. When Magnolia remodeled our interior, they attached ¼" drywall to the ceilings and almost all interior walls. Drywall is essentially compressed gypsum rock sheathed in two layers of thick paper. It has many virtues but is not very elastic and thus prone to cracking. This is important to keep in mind for anyone renovating an older home.

I vote for the long-term benefit even if it means more cost upfront. So, we invested in Mailander and tried to do the work the right way--sustainable over the long haul. In making our decisions for spending money to repair our old Mailander House, Marla and I talked a lot, with each other and our friends. I drew upon lessons I learned about business and investments, going back decades. Marla, too, had learned in the school of hard knocks. She had made a few good investments, and one, involving tearing down an old brick schoolhouse to scrap the bricks, was so bad that she still avoids discussing it. As the saying goes, Fool me once, shame on you. Fool me twice, shame on me.

Part IV   Mailander House Bed & Breakfast

Chapter 12   Making the Transition

When Marla and I have stayed in Airbnbs or other vacation rental properties, I thought the people who rented these properties were clever; they had found a legal way to get someone else to make their house payment! Marla and I discussed the possibility of renting rooms while we were living in the house, but decided we were not keen to have strangers, no matter how nice they were, stay with us because we value our privacy and intimate time alone.

Even though Marla loves me very much, there have been times when I think she wanted to kill me. One of these times was when I suggested that we move from Mailander House permanently. There we were, just settled into the house and working hard to pay for it. My brilliant idea was that we move to Marla's other house, Hound Haven, turning Mailander into a vacation rental, with the goal of paying off the property in five years.

Hound Haven is a modest but iconic house, built of stone and timber in 1930 by locally famous Gaines De Graffenried. Many of the rooms have been affectionately classified as true "man caves." Apparently, neither Mr. De Graffenreid nor his wife liked to cook, as the kitchen would be described as "primitive" by a charitable person. The house has a few problems beyond the primitive kitchen. In the backyard is a branch of Waco Creek that can flood during hard rainstorms. The flooding is most likely a result of the city allowing upstream building without planning for storm flow management. Consequently, the basement of Hound Haven, where the laundry equipment and hot water heater reside, has flooded on several occasions when the creek over-tops its banks.

At the time I proposed to leave Mailander and move to Hound Haven, it was occupied by a group of Baylor students who were renting until they graduated. The students were planning to decamp to other habitation in June, leaving the Hound empty. Therefore, we would not be homeless, living in our car, or worse yet, imposing on relatives, but we would leave the Mailander, which was in excellent repair, for Hound Haven, which had suffered from benign neglect. There was plumbing and electrical service, but both were about 90 years old and prime for replacement. (In fact, Hound Haven became another fixer-upper project for us as we have repaired many of its deficiencies. Maybe fixing old houses is a disease!)

So, why move? It was simple really, and we are not the only ones who figured this out; many people in Waco are now following in our footsteps. There is not a lot of news in Waco on some days, so anything related to Magnolia Market and *Fixer Upper* gets a story on the front page of the local paper. So, in January 2016, stories started to appear about the Magnolia House in McGregor, about 20 miles west of Waco. This is what the local paper, the *Waco Tribune* reported at that time, "More than 3 million viewers watched the holiday *Fixer Upper* special in which the Gaineses renovated the home at 323 S. Madison Ave., the highest viewership for an episode so far of the show's three seasons."

Subsequent *Waco Tribune* stories over the next few weeks reported on this financially successful venture. Articles stated that guests had booked an entire year's worth of stays in just one week online. The nightly rates at that time were $699 during the week and $995 for weekends (with a two-night minimum). I penciled that out and shared it with Marla. The gross income for a year was astonishing to us --$280K. All that booked, and presumably paid, in just one week! Because we had so many people coming by our Mailander House for a look and a few photos, I figured we should try to jump on that bandwagon too.

I soon headed out to McGregor to learn what I could about the new operation. I had the opportunity to chat with the on-site managers who lived in the smaller home behind the main rental house. These folks were very friendly and provided lots of information and recommendations, including the following:

- The guests generate a lot of laundry. Having an industrial strength washing machine and gas dryer is beneficial.
- The house must be squeaky clean.
- Guests appreciate the little things, that, while they do not cost much money, show the owner cares. For example, at the Magnolia guest house, guests were treated to fresh-baked pastries and high-quality coffee.

To these ideas we added a few of our own:

- No clutter. One of the great things about Magnolia-style is the lack of visual noise.
- Decor should conform to the theme of the house. Most people who know our *Fixer Upper* episode remember Chip and Joanna unpacking a vintage bicycle and putting it on the wall of my office. Therefore, we went with the bicycle theme, complemented by black and white photography and art generally appropriate for a 100+ year-old home.
- Good beds. People staying with us would be on vacation, which is a time to rest and recharge. We bought the best beds we could find – money was not an object.
- Provide lots of information to help first-time visitors.

Marla and I had some experience with home stays and non-hotel accommodations. I had spent a lot of time in guest houses in Nepal during a long spring climbing trip to the Himalaya in 1981. In remote mountain areas, it is common for travelers to buy meals from a family and stay in the house for a nominal fee. These home visits provided profound insight to the devotional Buddhist practices of the local people and how content they were with a simple life –no roads, no electricity, pretty much living as their ancestors had for hundreds of years. Despite the meager (by Western standards) accommodations, the Nepalese hospitality and caring spirit was always genuine and profound.

On subsequent trips later that decade, I had stayed in bed-and-breakfasts in New Zealand and Australia. Marla had done the same on her ski trips to Europe and Canada. In all cases, we had enjoyed meeting and visiting with our hosts and getting a taste of the local flavor. After Marla and I met, we stayed in an apartment managed by a wonderful Airbnb hostess in Buenos Aires. She provided us with lots of information about the immediate area, the city subway system, and tips for local restaurants and gardens. On a ski trip to Utah, we stayed at a small vacation rental apartment in Ogden and had an excellent experience. So, we were confident that we could create an appealing guest experience.

We knew that our Mailander House was attractive because it had been restored to much of its original beauty and was in a prime location for Waco visitors. We also knew that we could greet our visitors and provide them with a top experience. So, we decided to see if we could successfully turn Mailander House into a popular and profitable vacation rental. Other folks whose houses were remodeled on *Fixer Upper* were doing the same thing; a big rush of new vacation rental homes in the Waco area that started in 2016 continues today.

We knew nothing about managing a vacation rental. But we did know two things: We had to get the house ready, and it had to look sharp right from the start. It needed not only to pay for itself monthly, but also support our goal of owning it outright in five years. There was no way Marla wanted to give up her nice house if renting it was going to be a monetary black hole. We decided on a rational strategy. Marla and her office manager, Dotti, would manage home decoration – clearing clutter and capturing the Magnolia design spirit. I would manage the Internet side, getting good photos and writing up all the house information. I felt optimistic about this plan, but Marla was quietly seething. Apparently, in her previous marriage, her husband had had some 'great ideas' that got started but were never completed. She was concerned that I was cut from the same cloth and forcing her to move out of Mailander was going to be a huge pain with no gain.

    We got busy and by mid-June had a viable guest house offered on both VRBO and Airbnb. One of the crucial things required to get started are a few renter reviews. For this one, we cheated a bit. We offered the house to our friend Ydnar and his lovely wife Norahs. They came up from Kerrville, TX and stayed for a long weekend. Then, Ydnar wrote a comprehensive review of the house and their impressions. It was honest, direct, and positive. This helped us get some traction. We also priced the house at the lower end of the market to start, just to get folks in the door and show a rental history. This strategy worked, and in the first month we had $5,000 in bookings, and the next month $8,000 in bookings. This is not what Magnolia House did ($280,000 for an entire year booked in one week), but we are just regular people, not bonafide TV stars who could make the renovation of their home a centerpiece TV episode gaining the attendant publicity.

    Once Marla saw the money coming in, she started talking to me again; it had been quiet at the dinner table for a few weeks. I was allowed back in the house to sleep (I had been out back with the dog). She started to trust me a bit more. This is a natural process in any marriage: learning the true nature of a spouse and how they react to stress. For me, the challenge of proving we could do it was inspiring. I can really focus when I have a challenge, and I wanted to make my wife happy. We continued renting Mailander to guests, and it was usually a lot of fun. Of course, it took effort to do lots of laundry and keep the house super-clean. But it was also fun to meet the guests, help them get oriented, and provide ideas about fun places to visit. Sometimes they even left us little gifts of wine or flowers. In general, our guests were great and we were very happy to host them.

    We are not alone amongst the *Fixer Upper* people hosting folks visiting Waco via Airbnb and VRBO. Our friends Josh and Jill Barrett are renting their Mid-Century Modern very successfully. Other houses featured on the TV show that are currently vacation rentals include the Harp House, the Gorman House, the German Schmear

House, David Ridley's Bachelor Pad, the Barndominium, the Shotgun House, and the Chicken House. Each of these houses has its own unique identity. That is one of the fun things about staying at vacation rental properties managed by the owner; each one has its own personality that can reflect the builder and the current owner as well.

Chapter 13   Strategies for Success

My style was to greet guests at Mailander House and chat if they liked. I often asked questions to learn their interests and tried to provide information that could make their visit more enjoyable. Most guests liked to visit with me, as they had already seen me on TV, but I tried to focus on the house and how it fit into the bigger picture of central Texas history. Generally, our guests liked this approach.

When we started to rent Mailander House, I wanted to be as successful as I possibly could. Therefore, I threw myself into making our rental a going concern. I pored over many reviews of successful vacation rental properties on Airbnb and VRBO. It's easy to see who is doing it right by looking at their bookings for any given month. The good ones all had several things in common--cleanliness, quality beds and furnishings, and often, potential guest interaction with an engaging host.

So, over some months, I developed a fluid script for meeting and greeting guests at Mailander House. It went something like this:

> Local history is fascinating. The early Americans inhabited this area for at least 14,000 years before they were pushed out by Europeans. First the Spanish moved up from Monterey, Mexico in the late 1600s and English speakers came to the area in the mid-1800s. The Tonkawa Caddo people lived on the western bank of the Brazos River, where Mailander House is located, for good reason. First, there are several springs of fresh drinking water that arise from the limestone of the Balcones Escarpment, now called Proctor Springs and Indian Springs. Each is just a mile from where the Caddo people made their village, called by the Spanish, Quiscat, after their chief.
> The native people did not locate their village homes on the east bank of the Brazos, presumably because they had a long historic knowledge of floods on the river. The white people, having pushed the native Caddo up into the 'Indian Territory'

of what is now Oklahoma, apparently did not bother talking to the people they displaced. The white men built in areas that historically flood on the east side, with disastrous results. The Caddo peoples lived on the west side of the river where the bluffs are 75 feet or more above normal river level. Charles Mailander, being a wise and prudent man, built his house upon this high bank, far above the flood waters. Presumably Mailander had seen the flooding and damage in 1885 and chose the property on 5th St. for its favorable location.

My guests liked it when I explained why our house was built at its location, and why it has lived for 108 years when so many other houses have been torn down or abandoned. I also told some of our guests many of the stories included in this book. Many are parables about how to live a right livelihood, find one's place in a new community, and have a happy marriage, the latter being not only the icing, but the whole dang cake!

Chapter 14   The Bureaucratic Process

When we started renting our Mailander House on the Internet in June 2016, not many local houses were in the short-term rental pool yet. There were a couple of traditional bed-and-breakfasts, but not many of the current style: whole house rentals on a night-to-night basis. At that time, the City of Waco had an ordinance in place that was top-heavy with paperwork, and it took several months for an application to work its way through the bureaucracy. I'm not sure how the original ordinance came into being, but it was used in the past to block at least one high-visibility project for a vacation rental in a large stone house called The Cottonland Castle.

The Cottonland Castle, modeled after a small German castle, was built over several decades starting in the 1890s and used as a residence for most of its early life. Around 1969, it was purchased by the Austin Avenue Methodist Church, but the building was sold because of maintenance costs. Various subsequent owners have proposed repair either for a residence, wedding venue, or use as a bed-and-breakfast. All proposals to use the building for commercial purposes have met with large outcries of opposition from neighbors, so the building continues to sit empty and lacks needed repairs. Castle Heights, named after the Cottonland Castle, has always seen itself as a tony area for the upper crust to reside (it's right there in the original ads for the subdivision back in the 1920s). Many of the vocal folks in that neighborhood fall into the general category of NIMBY: Not In My Backyard. Of course, this is better than BANANA: Basically Absolutely Nothing Anywhere Near Anyone.

Knowing that some of the past city council public hearings had been ugly when neighbors opposed applications for bed and breakfast permits, I was leery when we got started with our vacation rental business. We made it a point to meet all our immediate neighbors, and Marla took care of some of their pets as well. Most of the nearby homes are owner-occupied, and we believed that our neighbors were quite pleased at how the old house on the corner (Mailander), previously something of an eyesore, was restored with fresh landscaping and regular care. This would be an asset, I hoped. I figured that if our neighbors knew and liked us, they would not oppose our proposal to make Mailander House a vacation rental.

First, I researched the legality of what we wanted to do. Waco has a modern zoning code that is easy to use. I determined that our zoning, "Office" or O-zone, would allow a vacation rental. In fact, our O-zoning allowed up to a five-story hotel or rooming house, along with many other business types. But, before I spent $300 on a permit application and started the legal dance at City Hall, I wanted to know if the business would be in the black. Therefore, for the first few months of operation, we flew under the radar and did not have a city permit. As it became apparent that Mailander House would be a viable vacation rental, I applied for a city permit with the planning and building department.

Planners at the city offices quickly became swamped with vacation rental applications as they were understaffed and not prepared for the growth propelled by Magnolia Market and the wildly popular TV show. Initially, it took months for applications to be processed and consumed substantial staff time. I attended many city meetings where it became apparent that the approval process was also very time-consuming for both the Plan Commission and City Council. As owners, a group of us went through a series of public hearings and got to know each other. I noted that when Chip and Joanna's Hillcrest Estate vacation rental was reviewed, they sent members of their staff - neither Chip nor Jojo appeared. The Gainses are on the down-low around Waco as much as possible, and who can blame them?

The hearings at City Council for several proposed vacation rentals in the Castle Heights neighborhood were heated. While the applications met all the requirements of the law and were approved by the plan commission, the city council backed down under extreme neighborhood pressure and denied the permits. A property near my sister-in-law, Gail, was denied a vacation rental permit after the neighbors raised a hue and cry, so a new owner just rented the property month-to-month to college students. Monthly rentals do not require permits or hearings.

Under Texas law, a property owner can rent a home to *anyone* for 31 days or longer; a city cannot require permits for this, and the owner does not have to pay special taxes. For a stay up to 30 days, cities can regulate the rental and charge special occupancy taxes. This is an oddity of law, and some of us just shake our heads. How does the difference between 30- and 31-days occupancy determine if a resident of a rental property is quiet and respectful or not? Many of the NIMBY opponents at hearings I attended sounded fearful to me. They must have missed that part in history class about FDR's famous statement that, ". . . the only thing we have to fear is fear itself."

Another element of the application process was the city's 'Life Safety Inspection.' Apparently, this is not performed on run-of-the-mill home rentals of more than 31 days; it just applies to short-term rentals. Essentially, we paid $75 for an inspector to spend about 10 minutes verifying that we had working smoke detectors, a carbon monoxide detector, a fire extinguisher, and wiring that met the building code. Mailander House passed with flying colors. Such a deal - we met all the requirements, could now have a permit, and would pay 15% in occupancy taxes. In truth, the guests pay the taxes as well as cleaning fees, but the owner must go through the process of monthly filings and payments.

As 2016 progressed with a flood of vacation rental permit applications, each of which had to be heard by both the plan commission and the city council (twice), the council had an epiphany. They realized that the current process was cumbersome to all involved and largely unnecessary. Therefore, an ad-hoc committee of planners and citizens was formed to streamline the process. The Waco City Planning Director is very sharp, and he and his team developed a regulatory package that simplified things for both applicants and staff. A few sections of the new regulation seemed unnecessarily burdensome, such as parking requirements, but the city council adopted the new code requirements and moved on. In fact, many of the requirements are only enforced if there are neighborhood complaints or other problems.

Chapter 15   Unusual Guests

By late 2016, we had a going concern with our Mailander House vacation rental. For the most part, our guests were wonderful folks who were very kind and thoughtful. But, as anyone who works with the public knows, some interactions are a bit unusual. I have already related the story of the 'Gas Leak Ladies' and what good sports they were; here are a few more.

Grass Roots Americans

One of our early bookings was a group of farmers from Toledo, Ohio. They drove down from Ohio through Waco and were headed to San Antonio for a farming conference. It was late winter, and they were quite pleased with our warm and easy weather. The group included two married couples in their 50s, and these folks were the salt of the earth. I enjoyed how they related to our old house. I told them that the Mailanders were builders and craftsmen, and this house had been built in 1910. Because my family was from Ohio and we were farmers, albeit in California, I felt a close connection to these folks. The ladies of course wanted to spend the time shopping at Magnolia Market, and the men generally relaxed, had a few beers, sat on the porch, and enjoyed the sunshine. I visited with them for quite a while, and I think we all enjoyed swapping stories.

This was shortly after Trump had been inaugurated and installed in the White House. He had threatened to apply tariffs on agricultural commodities, and I expressed concern for folks in the farm belt. These gentlemen grew specialty crops like popcorn and weren't much worried about tariffs or trade wars. I asked them about Trump's propensity to tweet frequently, and if they thought he was stable. They said it was part of his agenda to connect with his base, and thought he would be doing things to help our country. It would be foolish for a host to create an argument with his guests, so I mostly just asked questions and listened. My Dad used to say, "You can't learn anything with your mouth open."

The Toledo farmers were different from most of the guests we've had before or since. Most of our guests have been folks who wanted to connect with the magic of Joanna Gaines that they saw on television. These farmers were stopping in because they were on a road trip and it was a nice place to take a few days off from driving. I really enjoyed talking to the farmers about their homes. One couple lived in a house they had inherited which was originally built in 1848. They totally understood when I told them stories about our plumbing, electrical and foundation issues. Unlike some guests who didn't understand that in most old houses, bathrooms, closets, and people were smaller, these farmers from Toledo completely got it. They were very fresh and welcome guests.

American Fork Six Pack

Another of our early guests was a group of women from American Fork, UT. The town has experienced substantial growth since the 1970s, and when I have driven through on my way to ski Utah powder, I have noticed cookie cutter houses designed for large families. Family homes built today are much different than residences built in 1910. So, I had a suspicion that people from American Fork would not be ready for our old house. At that time, we were allowing groups of up to five guests.

I don't usually pry into my guests' personal lives, but these women were very communicative. They wanted to know how many showers we had. Our listing described bathrooms and didn't specify that we had one bathtub and one shower. The guests also wrote me an email asking if we had hair dryers. I started to suspect that these guests might be high maintenance. I warned the guests that we had two small bathrooms and it might be inconvenient for five women to put on their makeup, do their hair and get ready to be at the Silos by opening at 9 a.m.

No matter, they said they were game and wanted to stay at our house. Fine. When I met the guests upon their arrival, there were six women, even though our listing clearly specified five people maximum. I didn't have the heart to ask them to get a motel room, so I allowed the sixth person. I bet they were tripping over each other between using the bathrooms and the hair dryers and preparing themselves for their launch into the public shopping whirl. Immediately after this, I changed our listing to a maximum of four people, and enforced it politely, but strictly. We wanted our house to be a pleasant stay and not a college dorm party.

The review these guests gave us was quite interesting. They said something like, "We were warned, but we were still shocked at the size of the bathrooms." Well, honey, you weren't in American Fork anymore. This is Waco and a 108-year-old house. This crew will have a real wake-up call if they ever go to Paris, London, or Rome because plumbing is an afterthought that is bolted on to the outside of walls in many parts of those cities, and accommodations are often tiny by U.S. standards.

Popcorn Child

I was strict about not allowing children under the age of twelve because Mailander House has many small panes of glass near the floor. These small windows give the house a tremendous amount of light as they stretch up almost to the eleven-foot ceilings on the south and west sides of the house. Several of the interior doors were almost completely glass as well. This is mostly brittle old glass, probably from 1910, with visible waves in many of the panels. This type of glass was phased out for safety reasons, and modern glass is less brittle and shatters into very small pieces. Old glass shatters into large fragments shaped like knives or spears.

When I was about thirteen, a very tragic thing happened at a friend's house. My pal's older brother was in the kitchen horsing around with some of his buddies. While the older boys were messing around, one of them got pushed through a sliding glass door. That door was, unfortunately, of the older type of glass, and it shattered into knife-like shards. One of the shards penetrated deeply into the boy's neck and killed him. I well remember visiting a day or two afterwards and seeing the plywood that still covered the hole where the sliding glass door had been. There were also traces of blood on the floor from the boy who had been killed. I have never forgotten this incident, and it made me very cautious about renting Mailander House to families with small children.

The simple rules for our vacation house were clearly spelled out in the agreement that anyone booking through Airbnb or VRBO is required to accept. I had an interesting incident occur that created a conflict between my first goal (not to be a jerk), my second goal (protect small children), and my third goal (to make the guests happy). A woman from Louisiana had booked the house for herself and her two daughters. She emailed me and said they were going to visit the Magnolia Silos to do some shopping and "fun girl things." I thought, Gosh, this is my typical guest group, and they will have a nice experience.

Upon arrival, when I met the first two guests (the daughters) who drove up from Houston, I was quite nonplussed that a two-year-old accompanied the adults. I was polite to the ladies and asked them to come up on the porch where we could talk. Their mother, who had booked the house, had not yet arrived from Louisiana, as she was driving separately. I told the two younger women, the daughters, that small children were forbidden from staying at the house.

The mother of the small child took umbrage with this and started to become rather sassy and unpleasant. Having been around two-year-old children myself (as the oldest of six), I understood that she was probably a bit tired and was perhaps close to her wit's end. The last thing she needed to hear was that they could not stay in the vacation rental with her mom. However, I stuck to my guns and said "Hey, the rules are the rules, which you agreed to when you booked the house." The young mother told me it was my responsibility to contact them and tell them that small children were not allowed. Hmm, this was not pleasant; it especially bothers me when people do not take responsibility but want to make their failures my problem.

Basically, the young mother did not want to own the situation. This is never a good way to start a new relationship, and that's what we were doing. After about twenty minutes, the mother (also the child's grandmother) who had booked the home arrived. She was very pleasant and perhaps a little curious about why her daughters were not in the house yet. I took her aside and talked privately with her about the situation, explaining why the window glass was unsafe for small children. It turned out she was very busy with her job in the oil industry and had probably zipped through the on-line booking without reading the house rules.

Remembering that I did not want to be a jerk, I thought I could make lemonade out of lemons. I told the three women about my friend's brother and the death in the kitchen. I explained that the glass in Mailander House was very close to the floor at a perfect height for a two-year-old to go sailing through. I explained that I could easily replace the pane of broken glass, but I could not replace a small child. I explained I created rules to protect children and that I was very concerned about the active young girl they had brought with them. A compromise was reached, and all turned out okay. Because there were three women, I figured that one of them should always be able to keep an eye on the toddler. I made them promise me, cross their hearts and hope to die, that they would keep an eye on the toddler and keep her away from the window glass that could kill her.

After these guests left, I had an interesting housecleaning experience. It turned out that one of the ways they kept the toddler entertained was by feeding her sweetened popcorn. I found bits of popcorn in the rugs, in the couches and chairs, behind the beds, and under the desks. I have never cleaned the house so thoroughly, because popcorn (especially sweetened) attracts ants. Generally, when a group of three women leave the Mailander House, they leave it as clean or cleaner than they found it. In this case, I put my vacuum cleaner to good use with its strong suction attachment. Few things put fear into a vacation rental owner more than a potential ant invasion.

Where Is the Water?

These four guests were pleasant rural folks from the upper Midwest who had come down to Waco in the spring for some warm weather and shopping. These gals were farmers used to the challenges of old equipment and old houses. That was lucky for me, because I had a few more unexpected plumbing problems. On the second day of their stay, about 10:30 p.m., they called to report that the water was not working, and they could not take a shower or flush the toilet.

I had been getting ready for bed but zoomed down to the house to see what the problem was. I went into the basement, which is an easy way to access the crawl space under the house. Sure enough, there was water under the house and seeping into the basement as well. I crawled forward toward the front of the house through some thick mud to discover a pipefitting installed by the plumbers that wasn't just leaking; it was completely pulled apart. I shut off the water at the street to stop the flooding. I had some plumbing fittings in the garage and made what I thought was a very adequate fix. Well, my luck was not that good.

At 6:30 the next morning, just as I was fixing coffee, the ladies called me reporting they had no water and no way to shower or flush the toilet. Of course, I zoomed back over to the house to determine what the problem was. Sure enough, the same fitting was causing problems and was leaking so much water into the basement that there was nothing left to supply the showers or toilets in the house. Fortunately for me, this was a weekday and the plumbing supply store was open.

The ladies graciously gave me some time to get to the plumbing store, buy new fittings, and return to fix the broken water pipe. It was only a seven-dollar part, but boy did I get muddy. The bright side of this whole episode was that the guests were very considerate and compassionate and cut me a lot of slack while I fixed the water lines. Apparently, their husbands frequently grappled with the same problems on the farm. These are the best kind of guests to have.

Halloween Horror

I had an interesting crew from Boston book three nights, and they emailed me about how excited they were to stay in one of Jojo's magnificent creations and explore "Your fabulous city." Seriously? I don't know a single person in Waco who would describe this city as "fabulous." I've been to every US state and a lot of developed nations and can't think of a single American city that I can describe as "fabulous." Sienna, Italy is amazing; Kathmandu comes close to fabulous, but only in an edgy way; Waco, not at all fabulous.

I thought, okay, Boston gals, bring it on. I met these guests about 6 pm, let them in the house, gave them a wee tour, and then left them to their own devices. About 10 pm, I got a text message saying they had all fled the premises because it was, "Overrun by large spiders." Oh my. Not wanting to break my first goal or receive a bad review, I gave the gals their entire rental money back, less the cleaning fee, as they had taken showers and I had some laundry to do. The bummer for me was that I had lost the opportunity to book anyone for that three-day period, which meant I lost about $600 in income.

Mailander House has double-hung windows in many of the rooms. These single pane windows leak like a sieve around the edges so I had sealed them all up with caulk to make the house more comfortable. During our first winter living in the house, I could feel the north wind blow cold air into our bedroom, so this sealing was a priority for me. Given how old the windows are, there were tiny openings along some of the edges where, apparently, small spiders had made residence. Even tinier flying insects were attracted to the windows, and these spiders, whose webs were about the size of a quarter, were enjoying dining on the very small insects. When I stopped by the house the next day, I saw where the guests had stuffed aluminum foil into these small openings, put transparent tape over them - anything to stop the dreaded arachnid invasion. Of course, spiders are usually shy creatures who stay near their web. If the guests did not try to sleep on the windowsill, there was no way that one of those spiders could come near them.

Still, I needed to get rid of these tiny spiders. I poked around a window and saw one --it was smaller than a pencil eraser--a common house fly could probably eat it! But I remembered goal three: make the guests happy. Many people have allergies or health problems, so I didn't want to poison my guests with insect spray. Some of my guests have had cancer and compromised immune systems, so I wanted my vacation home to be salubrious for them. My solution was to buy elemental sulfur powder that could be sprinkled into the small openings around the windows. Apparently, spiders have a very good sense of smell and don't like sulfur. Eventually, I was able to convince the spiders that they would be much happier outside and the problem went away. For what it is worth, I also used benign inert compounds like boric acid powder to control ants and the famous Texas water bugs (aka cockroaches).

Broken Furniture

Marla loves antiques and old stuff, what other people might call junk. Because much of Central and East Texas was settled by small-holding farmers, a lot of old furniture and household materials are available in our antique stores. Before the advent of the farm tractor, farms were small (at least by modern standards). Because farms were of modest size and people needed to live close to their work, the central and eastern part of Texas is dotted with hundreds of once prosperous small towns. Today in these small towns, most of the downtown shops and many of the houses are boarded up; the farmers have died or left for city jobs. All those old farms originally contained furniture, kitchenware, and tools, much of which wound up in antique stores. This is one reason why Central Texas is red hot for antique hunters.

Thus, it was not difficult for Marla to furnish Mailander House with many period furniture pieces and decor. All the physical work required to maintain a farm meant that obesity was rare, so period furniture was built for much thinner (and often shorter) people. At Mailander House, we had three old Danish modern chairs in the front room. These had been loaned to us by Gail, who bought them with her 1937 estate house in Cameron Park. The chairs are teak and black leather and looked pretty good in the front room of Mailander House.

Our guests were a young couple from Houston. It was winter, just before Christmas, and a cold storm blew in, with temperatures in the low 20s and strong north winds. There is an applicable saying, "There ain't nuthin' between Texas and the Arctic Circle but a barbed wire fence. And it might have fallen over." Marla and I had taken ten days off and gone camping at Big Bend National Park to spend the Christmas and New Year's holidays. Our hospitality manager, Elizabeth, was handling things while we were gone. Elizabeth called us a few days before Christmas to tell us the guests had checked out early and furniture had been broken.

It turned out that the guests left early because they did not like the cold. Presumably people live in Houston for a reason--it's hot there! The woman had just given birth a few months before their visit, and Elizabeth said the guest weighed at least 300 pounds. Apparently, the woman was nursing the child in one of our antique Danish modern chairs and perhaps had a difficult time getting up. She broke a chair arm and damaged one of the legs, too. Fortunately, we were able to repair the chair, but we did withdraw all three of them from service at our guest house. At about $1,500 apiece, they were too fragile and valuable to remain, so they were moved to our front room at Hound Haven.

Bay Area Guests Vacuum Fridge

At Mailander House, we liked to provide a rich experience for guests upon their arrival. This included amenities guests would find in their own homes. Our goal was to be superb hosts, knowing this would help our business because we would receive favorable reviews and referrals. We were always mindful that our competition was hotels and other facilities that were perhaps less expensive but did not provide the richness and full benefit of staying in a unique home, perhaps one seen on TV! We also wanted our guests to be able to relax and enjoy a new environment that promised fun experiences.

We often had guests come from distant areas after making multiple plane changes, dealing with rental cars, and navigating unfamiliar roads; they were ready to relax when they arrived at our guest house. Therefore, we provided snacks such as nuts and crackers, cheese and fruit, wine and beer, juice, sparkling water, and of course, coffee.

Because my family is in the wine business, I know a fair bit about wine, and I wanted to provide beverages that were fun and perhaps a little different, yet would not break our budget. One of our hobbies is trying new wines and going after the best bang for the buck. Believe it or not, in blind tastings, the most expensive wine does not necessarily achieve the highest score. Therefore, we selected four styles of wine to offer guests: a sparkling wine, a dry red wine, a sweet white, and a dry white. We also had an assortment of beers on hand, many of them microbrews produced in Texas.

The coffee we provided was usually Keurig, because 70% of Americans drink Keurig coffee, and we also provided fresh-ground coffee from our local roaster, Apex (which also owns Dichotomy Coffee House on Austin Avenue). Amongst this array of choices, our guests would normally sample a few things that they might find appealing. Other visitors didn't eat or drink anything we provided because they preferred finding their own items while shopping at the Magnolia Silos.

We had a young crew visit from the San Francisco Bay Area who apparently were quite excited to find substantial snacks and beverages available at no extra charge. Those guests helped themselves to almost everything in the house, which surprised me when I arrived to clean after their departure. While they did vacuum out the fridge and cupboards, they also left a nice tip which was very helpful, especially when I went to the store to replenish supplies. This was a situation where we allowed our guests to avoid some time-consuming grocery shopping, and they were very thoughtful in return.

Fireplace Bike Ladies

When we bought Mailander House, I was surprised to see an old fireplace in the backyard that looked like amateurs had made it. It was a large freestanding edifice that appeared to be constructed with broken masonry, perhaps a patio or sidewalk that had been torn up, and included some odd bits of a strange red ceramic material. It was decorated with some interesting paintings reminiscent of Egyptian hieroglyphs. The chimney worked well, so we had some nice outdoor fires that didn't smoke everyone out the way a campfire can. It came in very handy during one two-day New Year's celebration, which centered around burning some sections of old dead trees that I had cut down the previous summer. My first inclination, to knock that beast down and send it off to a new graveyard, was wrong. The old fireplace was very cool, and I'm glad we kept it.

Most guests didn't make use of the large yard, patio, and deck at Mailander House. Some guests would sit out on the porch to drink, smoke, have a cup of coffee, or read in the evening, but most folks were tired of being outside when they got back to the vacation rental and just wanted to "chillax" inside. Perhaps this is because so many of us live in towns where being outside a building is just not pleasant, and we get out of the habit of sitting outside or even going for an evening stroll.

I loved it when our guests did take advantage of our yard and the nearby Brazos River Trail that Marla and I enjoy so much. One spring, we had a group of gals who made full use of our wood supply and outdoor fireplace. They also rode the bicycles we provided all over town and told me they had a great time. They enthusiastically brought chairs out to the fireplace in the evening, building a fire and enjoying a bit of wine. They even sent me photos of themselves on the bicycles and around the fire. I was so happy they were having fun! I used some of these photos on our VRBO and Airbnb listings. I really liked it when guests made full use of what we offered.

Baylor Mom on Holiday?

When we started Mailander House, we thought that most of our guests would be folks attending Baylor events (though we quickly discovered that most of them came to shop at the Magnolia Silos). In August, when school starts, the students all seem to arrive at once. Parents often want to be there to help their kids move in and get settled. With tuition, housing, books, and lab fees, it costs about $50,000 a year to attend Baylor, so we assumed these parents would not have a problem shelling out $250 - $300 a night for accommodations in an entire house. We were always happy to oblige them with a good place to stay and any assistance that they might need.

One of the most unique Baylor-related guests we had was a woman business owner from Massachusetts. She had recently inherited a successful business when her husband suddenly passed away, and she was trying to keep the business going by herself. However, she wanted to help her son settle in to his first year at the new school, so she needed some additional support, which we were very happy to provide.

The woman had several specific requirements for staying at our home. First, she needed high-speed Internet. No problem. Next, she needed a place to ship about a dozen boxes of clothing, bedding, linens, and other items her son would need for his first year in the dorms. Because Marla's clinic receives daily deliveries from UPS and FedEx, it was no problem for our guest to send shipments there. Marla would bring them to Mailander House within hours of arrival. Finally, this single mother needed a workspace where she could spread out her business materials and dedicate herself to operating her business remotely. My office (with the old bicycle on the wall) was the perfect place. When she was a little tired, she could enjoy gazing upon the rusty glory of our 1905 Velvet Road Racer bicycle (as I often did).

Funky Garden Mojo

Marla and I know all about golf courses. We know all about fancy yards manicured down to the scissors' edge of the grass. We know all about lawn ornaments and garden gnomes fresh from China. We also know how Mother Nature decorates wild places, which is more our style. We like to walk in the gardens of funky neighborhoods in Santa Fe, Portland, Tucson, Austin, Madison, and even right here in Waco. I love to take pictures of cool garden ideas and try to replicate them in a small way at our home.

Marla enjoys exploring in Cameron Park partly because of the debris left behind by previous inhabitants. Cameron Park was inhabited by a group of folks (including former slaves) looking for a cheap place to live in the Reconstruction era after the Civil War. Substantial old brick and metal debris is scattered in the park, mixed in with the poison ivy and snake habitat. We were cautious, but we enjoyed delving into the woods looking for old treasures and bringing them home to decorate the yard of Mailander House. Since Mailander House was 104 years old when we purchased it, the property also held a fair amount of old domestic material in the yard that had been buried by leaves and organic material. I have found some 200 old bricks buried in the lawn and flower beds, some of which came from the Corsicana Brick Company, which closed in 1916; we call these Corsicana Reds.

One autumn weekend we had a very elegant Baylor mom as our guest, a gardener from Houston. She suggested I needed to cut the grass in a gentle third-person way, "The grass needs to be cut." I know that cutting grass short is not healthy for the lawn nor the environment because lawnmowers create a lot of air and noise pollution. So, I tend to strike a happy place with my mowing so that the lawn does not look too shaggy but is also tidy enough. My guest probably lived in an area of Houston that employs professional lawn care companies that thrive on frequent mowing, blowing (and billing).

As I toured the Mailander yard with this lady guest, I showed her the native plants I had added and the oak trees I had started from acorns gathered from the venerable oaks in my neighborhood. As I described the various organic sculptures that Marla and I were creating from found objects, I think she started to understand. At first the yard looked strange to her: a bit of a hodgepodge with old bricks used for edging, found objects and random metal tools placed as 'décor,' and unusual native plants growing, not what is generally seen in gardening magazines. Our yard, though well-tended, did not have the tidy appearance that she was accustomed to in her neighborhood. (Actually, I find 'tidy' neighborhoods with their cookie-cutter yards about as interesting as looking at identical loaves of bread on a shelf.)

After about fifteen minutes of garden discussion and description, my Houston guest started to understand my ideas about organic decoration, native plants, and allowing man-made objects to flow between plants, stones, bricks and other found materials. By 'organic,' I mean something that flows naturally and creates itself in the mind of the gardener without a discrete plan or drawing. To me, using both natural and man-made hardscape items enhances the interest of any yard or garden area.

This lady stayed for about four days and enjoyed some of our comestible amenities, such as wine and cheese. To her credit, she left us a very nice bottle of Italian red that somehow found its way onto my table for a Sunday family dinner! It was tasty.

Florida Guests Play 'Let's Make a Deal'

To manage the house effectively, especially since I was doing most of the cleaning and laundry myself, we maintained a two-night minimum reservation. However, occasionally I would fit people in for one night, usually during the middle of the week. I had one guest who was especially anxious to stay for one night with her mother, reportedly a huge fan of *Fixer Upper* and our Mailander House. This daughter was bringing her mother to Waco for a birthday celebration, and she explained it would be the most amazing thing if they could stay at Mailander House for one night. She gushed extensively in emails about how much she wanted to stay at Mailander House for one night only, as the next night they were headed to Austin

It was a special birthday, so I thought I would work them in. "Fine, yes, you come and stay with your mom, and I'll meet you at the house. Just let me know when you'll be there." After I agreed to the one-night stay, this guest started emailing me, asking for a special price because they were just staying one night. I started to have misgivings. I did not want to go down this road. I understood that once I offered a special price to one person, I would have to start doing it for everyone, and my business model would be damaged.

I found the whiny tone of the emails beseeching me for a discount annoying. I thought I was already doing her a favor by breaking with normal protocol and allowing a one-night stay, and now she was working me on the price. She was becoming too precious. So, I held the line on the price; it was their choice since I was not holding their feet to the fire to stay at Mailander House.

When the guests arrived, they were courteous, and I tried to be accommodating and gracious, inquiring about their family and their travel to Waco. The guests quickly started walking around the house, finding fault and complaining. One of the taps in the back bathroom sink had slow water flow, and it took a little while for the hot water to get to the sink. This quickly became a cause for concern, and they requested to cut the price in half for their stay. They also complained that there were no curtains in the front room, which is obvious from the pictures that we had on the booking site they used, but they found it to be something they could use to try and barter me down on price.

It turned out these folks were from Florida, previously New York City, and it appeared that bargaining was part of their nature and almost a game to them. To me, renting Mailander House was not a game; this was my business, and I grew tired of their complaining and trying to work me down on price. Eventually, as I started to lose my patience (which was already thin after the whiney emails), I told them I needed to leave, that I had never experienced guests like them, and I wished them well. I was shocked by how rude and disrespectful they were. My feelings were hurt since I worked so hard to make the house welcoming and provide a wonderful experience for my guests. I started to wonder if I needed thicker skin.

About 10 p.m. that night, I received a call from Airbnb stating the guests had left and checked into a hotel, and they wanted a complete refund. I asked why the guests wanted a refund. The Airbnb people stated that the water flow in one of the bathroom sinks was not acceptable, and the guests were disappointed and wanted their money back. Prior to their arrival, the daughter was gushing about how much her mother wanted to stay; they could only stay one night; could I make a special accommodation for them; oh please, Mr. Morrow, let us stay. Then, they wanted a discount, and, after the private tour, they wanted all their money back. This seemed outrageous.

After talking to Airbnb, I threw my hands up in the air and agreed to refund their regular booking fee, but I did keep the $75 cleaning fee. It was the least I could earn for my troubles answering numerous emails and spending over an hour with them in the house. If anyone asked me to recommend these folks as guests, I would either decline to state anything, or I would give an unequivocal negative response.

Nature Lovers

We had a lovely couple from Wisconsin stay in the spring who were very much into nature and the outdoors. When they arrived, they quickly inquired about hiking opportunities in Cameron Park, where they could rent kayaks to paddle on the Brazos River, and where the best wildflowers were located. Fortunately, some local folks have used GPS to map almost all the trails in Cameron Park, so one can use Google Maps to navigate while they're hiking. Kayak and stand-up paddle board rentals are super easy, and I got them dialed in quickly. I sent them out to the west of us, towards Valley Mills and Clifton, for the best wildflower displays.

These folks saw that I had books on the coffee table about native plants, and when I mentioned that I was landscaping with many natives, they immediately asked for a tour. I was quite pleased to share some of my knowledge with them. Since gardening in Waco is tough with our weather extremes, I experiment and pay close attention to see what works (dead plants are a key indicator of what does not work). My first strategy was to plant three-to-five trees for every one I cut down. They loved the idea that I gathered acorns from large healthy oaks in our neighborhood, sprouted them in pots, and got them started in the yard. Oaks grow slowly, but can live for centuries. (I counted the rings of one healthy oak that was about 535 years old when it was cut down in 1968 to make a parking space, ironically in a town named Thousand Oaks.)

These guests were very interested that I was propagating plants that provided food for wild birds and butterflies. Waco is on a major bird migration route, and it can be entertaining to watch the different migratory birds enjoy plant shrubbery. The guests appreciated my story of the soiled laundry. One of my passions is minimizing energy use. The average American produces 700 pounds of CO_2 annually just drying laundry. Hence, I like to hang clothes out to dry on a line (like my mother did).

Well, one fine November day, I had sheets and towels out on the line strung between my back deck and a native tree behind the house. A flock of cedar waxwings had just enjoyed a veritable feast on some berries provided by a large native bush in my yard's back corner. As they reposed on the branches of the tree to which the clothesline was attached, their tiny digestive mechanisms kicked in, and they discharged voluminous purple matter onto the clean linen drying below. What a mess!

The goals of my short-term rental hosting experience were to avoid being a jerk, watch out for the kiddos, and provide some local knowledge. Beyond the regular tourists, we hosted folks who stayed because of a sudden death in the family, a wedding, or family reunion. In all cases, I have tried to be pleasant, follow the Golden Rule, and exemplify social graces. In the main, most of my guests also tried to emulate the same behaviors. I feel immensely grateful to have met so many nice people who decided to come our way, and we hope their stay at Mailander House was memorable.

Chapter 16   Reviews

Being part of the *Fixer Upper* phenomenon here at ground zero in Waco is interesting, to say the least.

Marla relates a story from her clinic that illustrates how some locals viewed the conclusion of the *Fixer Upper* series:

Today, a client came in with his dog and he said, 'I saw you today.' I said, 'Yeah, frozen in time. That was four years ago.' I said to him, 'Yeah, I see myself every time I go get my nails done at the salon because for some reason there's a constant loop of Season One, Episode 13. Some folks who love the show say, 'Oh my God, it's near the end.' [Referring to *Fixer Upper* being in its final season].

The client and I had a little discussion of what's happening now with **Fixer Upper**, *and he provided me with some insight. He had done some listening and looking, and he believed that after the Rachael Ray show, other television networks have been careful to limit the ability of television stars to personally capitalize on their role on TV. Rachael Ray has a line of cookware and multiple cookbooks, and she also has a line of pet foods. These pet foods came under legal scrutiny because they're supposed to be natural. Apparently, there is some ingredient in them that is unnatural. The point is, Rachael Ray existed before there was an understanding by production companies that putting people on TV and showing their families, what they do, and how they do it, has a great potential for delayed income.*

The next question I asked my client was, 'Well, where do you think things are going?' and the gentleman said, 'I think Chip and Joanna were glad to get out of a contract that limited their revenues.' I said, 'That makes sense. Limiting their revenues isn't ultimately a happy situation for the people involved.' So, the next question was, 'What will Chip and Joanna do next?' I told him I'd bet they'll do something worthwhile. Perhaps they're just normal people with normal lives who would like to live them, I added. So, we had a bit of a discussion about how a normal person lives.

I said, 'Chip and Joanna have five children. That means they need five times the amount of money as a person with zero children.' My client had a dog and at least one cat, both of which I care for, and we sort of chuckled about the cost of care for them. I said, 'I had one child, and I knew that was going to be a big expense.' He said, 'I didn't go that far; I have a dog and that was expensive enough; cats are cheaper.'

So, we laughed and agreed that, 'With five children, the good news is, we bet the show's not over.' His feeling was there will be another show, a next adventure, and that they are not through yet. I'm not sure, I don't know, my feeling was that they're normal people with normal aspirations and that includes a reasonable amount of privacy. So maybe the show's over. Maybe it's not.

(Currently the Gainses are creating a new network with Discovery Television. A network is far bigger than one simple TV program. If this is the case, Marla may have missed a beat.) We spent our fortune and a lot of sweat to restore our house, and believed that it turned out well. When the opportunity arose, we decided to try to emulate Chip and Joanna's success in the vacation rental business. However, when it became known that some in Waco decided to be copy-cats, the blogosphere blew up. According to an August 15, 2017 article in *Country Living* Magazine, it's one of the most controversial aspects of *Fixer Upper*: Rather than live happily ever after in their shiplap-filled farmhouses, some of Chip and Joanna's former clients have turned right around to resell or rent them out, seemingly capitalizing on the HGTV show's popularity and increased tourism to Waco. Now, after facing criticism for offering their homes as vacation rentals, Fox News reports that some couples featured on *Fixer Upper* are speaking out—and insisting the Gaineses 'don't have a problem' with what they're doing.

All praise and thanks to the blogosphere. I was not ready for the nasty emails we received subsequent to this article and others like it. This missive was a gem: "How can you be so rude to Chip and Joanna? They gave you a wonderful gift of a new home and now you are whoring the gift. What makes you so disrespectful of them?"

Wow, that was some question. I didn't even know that the noun, 'whore' could be turned into the verb 'whoring.' I did not want to get into a nasty exchange with this person, but I did a little research. The writer was a 50-something single man who lived in Maine, and I was certain that he had never been a guest at our home. Presumably he liked to watch *Fixer Upper* and was under the impression that the home remodels were 'gifts.'

After Marla and I bought the house for $34,000, we paid $65,000 to Magnolia for the remodel (which was a real bargain for which we are grateful) and we also kicked in about $5,000 to upgrade the kitchen appliances. As I have noted, the job really needed at least another $30,000 more to finish it out. I provided quite a bit of labor for some of the tasks as well. How this expenditure on our part was a 'gift' is beyond me. I responded to Mr. Whoring politely and invited him to come down to Waco and tour the house so that I could show him all the work we had put into our 'gift.' I wish he had taken me up on this, because it is very interesting crawling around under the house to view the plumbing and foundation work we did!

Several of our friends, among them Josh and Jill Barrett, needed to rent their *Fixer Upper* Mid-Century home to make ends meet. In their case, Josh had a good paying job that ended abruptly, and they had to rent their Mid-Century Modern house when they could, just to keep the bank from foreclosing. When they rented it to weekend guests, Josh and Jill stayed with relatives and lived out of a suitcase. This is just a basic matter of someone doing what they must do to get by until they can get a good job going again. I am happy to report that their fortunes are rising now. Hard work and faith pay off.

During this time, a woman from Yuba City, CA named Maggie Cooper reviewed Mailander House. She gave us one of five possible stars, with no comments or photos. She was never a guest of ours. Apparently, she had seen the *Country Living* article (or other publications) and just thought it would be good to hate on us. Remember Maggie, as it says in the King James Bible, Galatians 6:7 "Whatsoever a man soweth, that shall he also reap."

Another interesting review was by a journalist who did not identify herself as such when I met her at Mailander House to welcome her as one of our guests. She writes for the *Dallas*

Observer, a weekly tabloid, and she was part of a group invited by an ad agency to come down to review an automobile that Chip likes to drive. Someone at the ad agency thought it would be fun to put up the ten reporters in several of the *Fixer Upper* houses. This is what our guest from the *Observer* (sponsored by the ad agency) had to say: The Mailander House has three bedrooms, 1.5 baths and doors that have a hard time shutting. In fact, the bathroom door in my bedroom didn't close at all. The lavatory was the size of an airplane bathroom. I couldn't change clothes there or even move around. There was barely any room for your feet while squatting on the toilet. Reality-television celebrities have renovated the home, but it's still an old house. You walk on the wood floors through the home, and the squeaking floorboards remind you the home was built in 1910, when the population was just 26,000 and Waco was known nationally as the location of infamous lynchings.

All the things she said about the house are true. In fact, we believe that small bathroom she complained about was added after the Mailander House was built. There is an old outhouse pit in the back corner of the lot. Many young people who have not traveled much have no idea what a luxury modern American indoor plumbing really is. And the last part of her review seems like a malicious dig at Waco, referring to something tragic that happened 100 years ago, with all the perpetrators long dead.

Of course, along with the less favorable reviews and comments from people (some of whom hadn't even stayed with us), we also had our share of glowing reviews:

> What a treat to stay in this special little house. It is absolutely charming and so comfortable. Great location to visit all the Magnolia Farm activities and of course, we were able to find the episode on You-Tube to watch and connect immediately with all the sweet touches that Chip and Jo as well as the owners made to really enhance the house. Would highly recommend!

Another group of women who stayed commented:

> We had a girls' trip in Waco during November and the house was a great home base (from which) to explore! The kitchen was well equipped; the living room was a great place for hours of girl talk and laughter; the beds and linens were comfy; the drive to almost anything was under 5 miles. We do a different location each year but if we were to go back to Waco, we would select this property again!

Mother/daughter guests said:

> The Mainlander was a great rental to relax and enjoy with family or friends. We did a mother daughter trip to Waco. During our stay, we enjoyed the quaint little house with big character. Loved the authentic designs, trying to keep it close to the original style. We all slept well. The house was very clean and well kept. The mattresses were very comfortable. It was easy to drive to downtown and other places of interests.

And a family reunion group said:

> We had a great two-night stay here -- great location, nice neighborhood, and David was an amazing host! He met with us at check-in and gave us lots of information about Waco and the history of his home. We loved that it was on *Fixer Upper* {heart}! We created many great family memories here on our family spring break 2018. Thank you, David, for your hospitality -- for sharing your amazing home with us and for the banana bread, fresh farm eggs and wine!

The comments we received were overwhelmingly positive; many guests reported that "The place was great, and the memory of staying at a fixer upper will last a lifetime!" Creating good memories for our guests really made this a dream job. Cleaning and caring for the house meant I was on duty seven days per week, but I benefitted so much from the kind words and interaction with our guests. As I said before, I can't make someone happy, but I was able to create the conditions for them to share joy with friends and family. This was a dream job that went far beyond the income generated.

Part V Dave's Previous Experiences

Chapter 17 Youthful Challenges

Along with many of my pals in high school, I worked for a Thousand Oaks landscape gardener we called the Mole Man. We learned a lot from him about plants, people, and business. He was smart about plants and terrible about business, always on the edge of going broke and equipment always on the fritz; he didn't even send monthly bills to his clients. However, Mole Man was usually patient and took care of us as employees. He was amused by us and how suggestible we were. Once, at a donut shop in Simi Valley, he paid for a contest among the lads to see how many donuts we could eat in fifteen minutes. Of course, the pain came when we, the gluttons, had to use a push mower on the three-acre lawn at the trailer park village down the street. Maybe this is why I am still not a big fan of large lawns!

Subsequently, I put myself through college working like an Irishman--my shovel and wheelbarrow were steadfast companions. One long summer during college, I worked for a brick mason. My job as tender was to carry bricks and cement blocks, mix mortar, and deliver it to the bricklayer. In the trade, this job is called 'hod carrier.' I learned that a wheelbarrow of fresh concrete can weigh up to 450 lbs. when I tipped one over on a customer's driveway. I quickly discovered that a wheelbarrow half-full means more trips but far less danger of creating a spilled cement mess. Carrying hod was some of the hardest work I have ever done, and it is an understatement to say that it motivated me to study diligently in college. I wanted to have employment choices beyond manual labor.

At the University of California at Santa Barbara, I picked up work with local contractors who needed a laborer and could accommodate my class schedule. I first worked for an Italian brick mason doing high-end work, such as artistic fireplaces. Then, I worked for a remodeling carpenter, Sugey Otis, who taught me a lot about building and rebuilding. Santa Barbara has some beautiful old homes and we worked on several of them over a few years. I was just a grunt and no one asked my opinion, so I just kept my mouth shut and observed.

One of the biggest problems I saw on remodeling jobs were customers changing their minds mid-way through the work. This usually causes the remodeling to drag on and on. For instance, on one job, Sugey had me spend several days disassembling old double-hung windows, restoring the counter-weights, and then reassembling and reinstalling the windows. A few days after I finished, the owner decided to remove all the windows I had just repaired and replace them with modern windows. Obviously, it cost the owner more money to do the windows twice. And, to make it worse, some customers had the temerity to complain about our labor bills when their own changes/indecision caused the cost overruns. One of the nice things about writing the checks is that owners can blame their own poor decisions on the workers. It felt demeaning to be blamed for owner-caused cost overruns, but sometimes that is the name of the game when working for rich people.

My most interesting work in the summer of 1977 was building foundations for airplane hangars at the Anchorage airport. In southern Alaska, perimeter foundations must be at least five feet deep, with all the concrete tied together by rebar. Because the ground freezes deep into the soil during winter and water expands about 4% when it freezes, the ground into which the foundation is built will expand and force it up toward the surface. This 'frost heaving' can play hell with building foundations and the structures that sit on them. The solution is to dig deeply and place the bottom of the foundation below the level of frost, so that the lower foundation will act like an anchor when the upper part is subject to frost heaving. Of course, the entire foundation had to be well designed and implemented with good-quality construction.

What this meant for me, a grunt, was that a backhoe came in and dug deep trenches. We grunts would then use our trusty Irish shovels to clean out the loose dirt, then tie rebar at various levels in the trench. Finally, we would insert plastic-coated heavy plywood forms into the sides of the trench to control the flow of concrete. After some days of preparation, a concrete truck would arrive to pump concrete into the trenches that we had prepared, burying the rebar deep within the concrete. It was pretty satisfying to see all the work completed after the concrete hardened. Subsequently, other masons would tie in to our steel perimeter foundation and pour a concrete slab floor. Finally, the building contractor would erect a metal building for the airplane hangar. We called modern concrete "liquid rock," so in our own way, we were following the gospel when we built those foundations.

Chapter 18   Family Ranch

When I was about 28, my family convinced me to come work for them at a new business they were starting near Paso Robles, California. My stepmother had inherited some money and wanted to start a wine grape vineyard. The ranch they bought included an old house, and during the rainy winter of 1982, I did a lot of work on that house with my cousin and a few friends. The work was pretty basic--new wiring and insulation and fixing some problems with the foundation. It was not a huge job, but it let me see how an old house can be rebuilt and improved rather than just demolished.

My folk's ranch was originally farmed for small grains, such as barley and wheat. I was assigned to live in the old farmhouse while I planted the new vineyard. The house had a couple of bedrooms and one bathroom, and a door in the bathroom led outside. The former caretaker advised me that I would have to remove that outside door every month and trim the top so it would open. Apparently, the house was sinking in that corner. My stepmother looked at the situation and said that I could have $5,000 to "fix the house." Apparently, part of the tax code allows farmers to deduct spending up to $5,000 to repair farm housing. With that small budget, I started crunching numbers. What would we need, and what could we do with available funds? (This was the same situation we faced thirty-five years later with Mailander House).

I had my old pal and carpenter, Sugey Otis, come up from Santa Barbara for an assessment as he had far more experience with foundation work. The first thing he did was to pull up some flooring in the area that was sinking. This allowed us to see that the ground was wet; the bathtub was leaking at the drain area, which kept the soil saturated with moisture year-round. Additionally, the house foundation consisted only of flat stones with boards laid on top. We later learned that the house had been moved to our ranch from another location, and the builders skimped a bit on the foundation (the part no one can see). Constant moisture from the leaking bathtub drain had allowed rot to set in, with moisture also moving up into the walls. This was a classic case where water and housing lumber don't mix.

In the winter of 1982 - '83, California experienced a strong El Nino winter with substantial rain. Our first task in the new vineyard was designing and installing the irrigation system, but with all the rain, it was nearly impossible to do any farming work because the fields were thick with black mud. We tried to go out into the field a few times with our new four-wheel drive Kubota tractor, which led to comical disaster. As the saying goes, four-wheel drive only allows one to go farther before they get stuck. So, we decided to work on the house instead.

There was a small recession under way at that time, I was able to hire a few under-employed construction workers, one of whom was Sugey and another my cousin Stevo. Four of us wound up working on the house while living in it, which in a wet winter was a bit rough. We had to prop up the roof and ceiling with temporary posts while we tore off two exterior walls, poured concrete foundations, and then rebuilt the walls. For a few days we only had blue tarps to keep the rain out, and it was more like camping in a big tent than living in a house. Thankfully, down sleeping bags and a big old wood stove kept us going. We also had a lot of fun in the evenings when Stevo played his banjo as we sat around the stove.

While we had the house exterior walls apart, we took off all the original interior paneling and rewired the whole structure to make it safer. Interestingly, we found old newspapers from the 1890s that had been put up under wallpaper, presumably to stop wind drafts. The exterior walls were just shiplap boards, so we insulated with fiberglass roll batting and then buttoned it up. We also insulated the attic, installed new windows, hung drywall, taped, and painted, making the place very solid. Although it only had a wood-burning stove for heat, I spent some 20-degree nights in that renovated house quite comfortably. I felt sad when I learned that lightning caused a fire and that old house burned to the ground a few decades later. As it is written, "Ashes to ashes, dust to dust."

Chapter 19   Behind the Redwood Curtain

My next big house project was moving a building at my house near Eureka, CA. That property had three buildings -- the main house and two garages. The garage next to the house had badly cracked concrete floors, so I decided to pour a new slab about 40 feet away and move the building to it. Because the soil in that area was subject to shifting, and there was an earthquake fault nearby, we put a lot of steel into the slab and made the concrete about 50 percent thicker than the required minimum. Since the old garage that we were moving was unfinished, we decided to make it into a regular living space that would be part office and part laundry.

After installing a small wood stove for heat, we wired it to modern code, insulated, hung drywall, and painted. It became a cozy office/guest room that served us well for many years. On that project, I also built my first outdoor shower, which was popular in summer, especially since it was right off the laundry area. I had many a muddy mountain bike ride that ended at that shower/laundry.

Eureka is "Behind the Redwood Curtain" because it is far from a large city. It is about five hours north of San Francisco and just south of the Oregon border. Set right on the Pacific coast, some areas behind the Redwood Curtain see up to 100 inches of rain annually. During major storms that sweep out of the Gulf of Alaska, up to 20 inches may fall in a single day. I worked for a local civil and environmental engineering company that did a lot of work designing drains and flood control systems. The small house I bought was inland from the coast to get out of the fog line that hangs along the beaches. This house had large second-growth redwoods flourishing on the property, testament to how much it rains.

My first winter living there, I noted how the downspouts for the gutters dumped right onto the ground next to the house. I thought this was odd, but shrugged, telling myself that was how things were done in this area. Once, while working under the house, I noted how wet the soil was. Why was there water under my house? There was no leaking plumbing. It was easy to assume that the downspouts dumping right next to the foundation were the culprit. But the house was not that big – just one bedroom, one bath - not a very large roof area to collect water, and there was a lot of water under the house. This was a bit of a mystery.

That same winter I decided to transplant a couple of cherry trees in the yard, which looked unhealthy from too much water. The root crown that interfaces between roots and trunk needs to be dry for most trees. Additionally, most fruit tree roots respire gases such as oxygen within the soil, and usually do not flourish when submerged in water. I built soil mounds for the cherry trees several feet above the lawn, and prepared spots for transplantation. I dug them up and moved them to their new, elevated homes. When I took the first tree to its new spot and then returned to fill the hole in, the freshly dug hole was filled with water. It had not rained for a couple of days and here was water-saturated soil just a few inches below my lawn. Ugh! High groundwater levels will deprive the roots of many plant species of oxygen, "drowning" the plant. But why was there water right near the surface out in the yard?

We lived on a small road in a community called 'Sunnyside' about ten miles northeast of Eureka. We were at the bottom edge of coastal hills ranging up to 2,000 feet high. Just across the road from my house was a steep hill of about 100 feet. Only later did I learn that this hill was an uplift from the earthquake fault line just a few hundred feet south of our house! As water likes to do, rain that fell on this hill absorbed into the soil and then migrated toward the creek below my property. Since my house was between that hill and the creek, I deduced that I had an underground current slowly working its way under my house. What to do?

After consulting with a couple of engineers at work and a pal who is a landscape architect, I devised an extensive French drain system to keep the house foundation dry. French drains are widely used in agriculture to protect crops from drowning and to prevent mineral salts from poisoning the soil. The technique involves determining and mapping elevations and then digging a sloped trench to move water toward a marsh, stream, pond, lake, or river. This encourages water to move from saturated soil into the trench and then flow downhill. To keep the water flowing, the trench is traditionally filled with small stones and gravel. A modern twist is to add a four-inch perforated pipe at the bottom to keep a nice clear space for the water to move quickly. The perforated pipe is often covered in a plastic mesh tube to minimize infiltration and clogging by soil and grit. The trick is to have enough water velocity to keep the pipe clear.

My buddy and neighbor Mike and I worked on many house projects together. When we weren't riding our bikes together, we were working on our houses. Mike also had some drainage problems at his house just up the street. We decided to tackle this drainage challenge together. First, we did some measurements and figured out the best ways to set the pipes to move water quickly through the French drain. We decided to tie our respective houses' gutters and downspouts into the drain that ran toward the same small creek that flowed in our respective backyards. In a heavy rain, a big pulse of water from the gutters would flush out accumulated soil that had worked its way into the perforated pipe. We had to order quite a bit of perforated pipe and screen material. My system alone was the length of a football field, and we were able to get contractor prices because we bought so much material.

The next step was to rent a big two-man trencher. We called it 'The Brute,' as it could tear a man's leg off if it got away, so we were very careful while operating it. Mike and I would wrestle The Brute into place and then start its powerful and very noisy gasoline engine. We tore through the soil, striking fear in gophers and worms alike; the only thing that stopped us were giant redwood roots. It seems the people who built our houses had just pushed dirt into place after the first growth of ancient redwood trees was logged. The big roots were still under there after 100-plus years; redwood contains tannins that inhibit rot. When The Brute would stop due to a large root, Mike and I would tug it out of the way and attack the roots with hatchets and axes.

Because this French drain was an optional project (not mandatory like the sewage break at Mailander several decades later), we chose to work in late summer when rain was unlikely. It took us several days of trenching and root hacking to get all the lines dug. The next step was to make sure the trench slope was correct: we didn't want hills and valleys – just one straight shot. We used a long 2x4 and bubble level for a whole day, digging and filling to get the trench slope just right. We even tamped the bottom dirt tight to make sure there would be no shifting. Then we set the drain pipe, working from the house downhill toward the creek, covering each 20-foot section with the plastic mesh. Then, we were ready to attach the gutters and downspouts to the drain pipe.

The final step was not as bad as I had feared. In it, the builder covers the buried pipe with small rocks and gravel to provide extra drainage and prevent soil infiltrating into the pipe. By this time, I was on a friendly first-name-basis with my local gravel company (from other home projects), so I had them bring out a ten-yard truck load, tip half the load onto my driveway, and the other half went to Mike, three houses up the creek. Since we were real men of Irish descent, we owned large metal wheelbarrows and had shovels aplenty. For the next week, each of us toiled away in our spare time like coal miners, pushing loads of heavy gravel around our lots, backfilling the trenches we had just dug. But it was satisfying work because it was a one-time proposition.

After this project was done, we threw a big outdoor end-of-summer oyster grill and party. I amused myself quite a few times the following winter by observing the water flowing out of the French drain at its terminus into the creek. When it was raining hard, it would really gush, but even a week after a heavy rain, the subsurface drains toiled away, capable of filling a one-gallon bucket in a minute. The dandy things about French drains is that they should work for an indefinite time with little (if any) maintenance.

Chapter 20   Dad's Fresno House

The story of this house restoration has an emotional component. About 40 million adult Americans are currently caregivers for an aging or ill person, so I hope this part of the story resonates with them. After my dad and stepmother split up, Dad, who had health problems, moved to Fresno to be near Colby, my sister. Colby, whose full-time job involved lots of travel, helped with Dad as she could. But eventually his healthcare problems became too much, and she asked me for help.

Dad's health was going downhill fast, and he needed regular medical care. As with many independent older people, he tried to carry on living alone, but things were going badly. Dad was used to making his own decisions and did not want to cooperate with some of the things we did to try and help him. There came a time when we had to call in the social workers and an attorney or two. It was not pretty or fun, but it had to be done; he had no Plan B when his health and self-care ability started to go south.

Because he had difficulty maintaining safe blood sugar levels, he occasionally blacked out, and his diminishing mental capacity courted disaster. After several scary incidents behind the wheel where he could have killed himself or someone else, I convinced him to surrender his driver's license and obtain a state ID card. Unfortunately, this didn't stop him from driving, and later a state trooper found him unconscious on the side of the freeway. He had been trying to drive to the emergency room. At this point, I became very concerned about him.

Some emotional blows followed. That winter, Dad became very ill with a pancreas infection. After he didn't respond to my sister's calls, she found him at home, barely able to talk, and rushed him to the VA hospital. It took him a month to recover, and then he had to live at a rehabilitation facility for a while. He was angry that he could not leave the hospital and take care of his suffering the quick way (suicide). He did not have the mental capacity to see the causes and conditions that had led him to where he was. I was very sad about how far my dad's life had degraded, and it was difficult to endure his anger with those of us trying to help him. I had one or two good cries after he and I argued about his desire to commit suicide. He was not pleased that I had taken away the pistol he bought for this purpose.

The Veterans Administration has a modern large hospital in Fresno, and dad was using their services, along with those of his family doctor. He had always been able to care for his own medical needs, but by 2012 he required serious medical care. He was not able to manage his diabetes medication and had repeatedly made trips to the emergency room, usually due to blood sugar crashes. He did not understand the heart medications he was taking and did not manage them well, so he was in-and-out of the hospital for several months. Finally, after three trips to the emergency room in one month, the county social worker came and spoke with him. She told him that the county senior services would appoint a conservator to manage his affairs if he could not get family help within thirty days. Dad finally saw the light and realized his family, who had been pleading with him to be allowed to help, could be a better alternative than a social worker (who probably had a massive caseload and would not be around much).

For several months, I made weekly 320-mile round trips from San Luis Obispo, where I was teaching, to Fresno at random times when Dad needed help. I finally decided to move to Fresno, commuting to work in San Luis Obispo. Fortunately, at that time my teaching load was mostly Tuesday through Thursday, so I could spend four days in Fresno each week. We moved Dad to a care facility for a while so that he could get his health back and learn to manage his own medications.

Dad's house was a disaster. He had not been able to maintain it, and large sections of ceiling had collapsed in the master bathroom from rain saturating the rotten roof. Other rooms had dead rats and toads in the closets. Dad had become a hoarder in a big way. One of his hobbies was buying food at a local grocery outlet. His garage and cupboards were overflowing with canned and dried food, much of it well past the expiration dates. He had a stand-up freezer in the garage filled with frozen meat, while the kitchen refrigerator was stuffed full, too.

Roof rats had taken up residence in Dad's garage and eaten any and all plastic or cardboard food containers. The summer heat in the garage had caused many food cans to go bad; I don't need to go into more detail. The carpet in the house was filthy beyond description. The cobwebs were so bad that our friend Dave, a house appraiser, came in and said, "I don't think I could create a haunted house with this décor no matter how hard I tried." Just the smell usually drove people out within a few minutes. I remember Colby gagging and leaving after just five minutes. I wore an N95 mask the first few weeks to avoid inhaling the dust, cat hair and unknown biota exuding from the carpet. I am certain that living in this environment contributed to Dad's ill health.

Dad could not repair the house, and no one else in the family wanted it in such a state, so he signed it over to me. It was my first real 'fixer upper,' where I paid all the bills and took all the risk. This experience would serve me well in Waco (although I did not know that at the time). After the major triage I did on Dad's house, nothing related to home remodeling could phase me in the future. While Dad was in the hospital for a month with his pancreas episode, Colby and her husband Evan came over and helped me sort Dad's belongings, storing the good stuff.

I now owned a 1985 ranch-style tract house that had blue tarps on the roof and was uninhabitable. The yards, front and back, were badly overgrown and looked awful from the street. I made a list of all the things that needed work and did some cost estimating. I probably spent an entire week doing research at hardware stores, looking at home remodel books, and searching the Internet. I had no idea how many hours of work were ahead, but I took about $30K out of my retirement fund and got to work. There was so much accumulated trash and hoarder debris that the first thing I did was order a 20-yard trash bin and have it placed on the property.

One thing I wanted to do with the house repair/remodel was make the home as eco-friendly as possible, saving money while making the house comfortable. There were several reasons for this.

First, I wanted to be proud of the work at the end of the job. If I cut corners, it would only reflect badly on me. I am not a big churchgoer, but I do believe in the Golden Rule as words to live by. I knew I would sell the house eventually, so I wanted it to be as good as we could make it given the resources available. A few years later, I saw this same dedication to 'doing it right' in the Gaines's and their Magnolia Homes work projects. This affinity has given me great satisfaction as I've watched Magnolia succeed on many levels.

I hired a few guys to help with the heavy lifting tasks, such as pulling up all the carpets. While we were mucking out the inside of the house, I started getting bids for a new roof. Fresno, being in the Central Valley of California, well inland from the Pacific Ocean, is quite hot for about six months of the year. I chose a type of light-colored asphalt shingle that has heat-reflecting beads embedded in it, a so-called "cool roof." I had an experienced roofing company do the work because I had no spare time to do it myself due to the attention required on the interior. I can highly recommend cool roof shingles to any fixer upper people living in hot areas--they really do work. These shingles kept the house at least five degrees cooler inside on hot summer days. This translates into lower utility bills and more comfort. Because most electricity is still generated by fossil fuels, it also lowers one's personal contribution to air pollution. I'm all about saving money while doing the right thing. I'm sure the neighbors were glad to see the blue refugee tarps removed.

During this time, I had a lot of mental stress due to the combination of trying to help Dad with his healthcare, perform my teaching job, and restore the old house. I also tried to squeeze in time for a certain Texas gal as well. To keep myself going, I printed this poem out and put it on the bathroom mirror so I could read it each day while shaving or brushing my teeth. It is important for me to start the day with "right intention."

When the Shoe Fits

Ch'ui the draftsman
Could draw more perfect circles freehand

Than with a compass.

His fingers brought forth
Spontaneous forms from nowhere. His mind
Was meanwhile free and without concern
With what he was doing.

No application was needed
His mind was perfectly simple
And knew no obstacles.

So, when the shoe fits
The foot is forgotten,
When the belt fits
The belly is forgotten,
When the heart is right
"For" and "against" are forgotten.

No drives, no compulsions,
No needs, no attractions:
Then your affairs
Are under your control.

You are a free man.

Easy is right. Begin right
And you are easy.
Continue easy and you are right.
The right way to go easy
Is to forget the right way
And forget that the going is easy.

Chuang Tzu [12th century][2]

---

[2] Tzu, Chuang. "When the Shoe Fits" from *In the Dark Before Dawn: New Selected Poems of Thomas Merton*. New Directions, 2005.

After repairing the drywall ceilings that had collapsed in the master bath, I hired a few helpers and we blew R30 insulation over the tops of the old insulation into the attic. Home remodeling tip: If customers buy the materials at a big box store, they will often let them use the insulation blowing machine free for twenty-four hours. The combination of the cool roof shingles and the thick attic insulation made a huge difference on the house's interior summer temperature, and I knew that would save me money on my heating and cooling bill. While re-roofing, we also added three solar tubes to light the kitchen, master bath and a hallway; what a difference! We popped a cheaper skylight in the garage, which helped brighten that area substantially. I retrofitted all the lights with modern energy efficient bulbs and fixtures. This was, in part, to save me money, but it would also make a difference when it came time to sell the house.

Within a few weeks of owning the house, I bought a chainsaw and dropped some trees that were growing right next to the house foundation. My brother Rico helped me take down a large tree that was shading the back roof. Why? Because I wanted solar photovoltaic panels. Fresno has more than 300 sunny days/year, so using solar makes sense. California has special electric meters that run backward (subtracting money from the bill) if a solar system is putting power back into the grid. The utility will even pay for this power if the solar system supplies more than used over the course of a month. My roof was not designed for solar, so the number of panels I put in was limited, but I was still able to save over $1,000 a year on electricity. Having this solar system helped me to sell the house very quickly a few years later.

While the roof was being repaired and new shingles installed, I fixed the garage door along with the gutters and the perimeter of the roof. The stucco paint was decent – it just needed power washing, but I found and replaced some rotten trim boards. Then, all the trim got a couple of coats of paint that matched the work I had done on the garage door. For a month or so, I lived in the house with bare concrete floors. It was kind of fun and easy to clean, but I knew it would not make for good resale. Consequently, I got bids and chose to install a faux-wood laminate floor from Home Depot. Carpet may be cheaper in the short-term, but it's bad news for anyone with pets or allergies (like me). I wanted a house that I could keep super-clean and allergen free, and the new floor gave the house a fresh look.

I had the HVAC system professionally inspected and serviced. It was older, but still working well, so we left that alone. Increasing the insulation and improving the exterior door sealing put less strain on the system, which made it more efficient. The older gas water heater looked like it could start leaking any time, so I replaced it with a high-efficiency unit. We scraped the popcorn off some of the ceilings because there were water stains from the leaking roof. One secret I learned was to wet everything down lightly before scraping to keep the dust down. We painted every room, including the ceilings.

When I was not working inside, I worked on the yard, which had been neglected for many years. I put that chainsaw to work and hauled loads of branches to the curb, as the city offered bi-monthly brush pickup. Colby's husband, Evan, and I made many trips to the Salvation Army thrift store, the local food pantry (to donate salvageable food), and, as a last resort, the landfill. Evan also did yeoman's work to help me get rid of the rats and their leavings; we went through a lot of N95 respirator facemasks that summer.

Because my sick dad had been so poor at medication management, there were pills spread all over the master bath counters. Now, with the help of kind medical personnel, he was slowly getting better at the VA hospital, so we figured he might need these meds at some point. A nurse friend came over one afternoon and helped sort out what could be used and what had to go. We packaged up what could be used or stored. I gathered up the remaining hundreds of pills and took them to the local police station where there is a safe medication disposal facility. I knew from my work at wastewater treatment plants not to flush them down the toilet. Most drugs are not broken down by municipal wastewater systems. They wind up being discharged right into groundwater basins, or into the ocean. Putting things down the toilet does not mean they leave the planet!

Dad's kitchen, to put it mildly, was a disaster. I retrieved enough diet soda aluminum cans from under the kitchen table to earn $22 at the local recycling center. Dad had spilled some disgusting substances on his beautiful antique maple kitchen table, but we were able to clean and restore it. My sister came over and spent a few balmy afternoons with a Chore Boy, applying massive elbow grease to the wood cabinets. The scrubbing was hard work and slow going. By this time, a normal person could breathe without an N95 mask. My dad apparently loved to fry things. We knew he used a lot of heat because of all the burned pans, so the grease smoke was probably intense, as evidenced by the spider webs that had absorbed the airborne grease and become stuck to the kitchen cabinet wood. It took a LOT of scouring to remove the greasy webs and restore the cabinets. I was able to salvage the dishwasher and refrigerator, but wound up replacing the stove, as the spilled food and grease was impossible to clean.

Dad had inherited some nice furniture from his mother, but over the years, it became damaged. He had a dust-proof bureau that was at least 100 years old. The drawers had a special type of dovetail joining, and one of them was broken. Another beautiful small primitive table was made of tiger-stripe maple. This little table was constructed before the American Civil War, a true antique. In one of his diabetic blackouts, Dad had fallen against it and broken it. I did not want to put these items out on the curb because they had been in the family for at least three generations. I did some research and found a local craftsman who worked from his home repairing and restoring furniture. He was not inexpensive, but did excellent work, and the $500 needed to restore these two pieces was money well spent. My sister Colby has them now and hopefully is enjoying them, and she will be able to pass them along to the next generations.

After we finished with a lot of the major work on my dad's place, I was sleeping in the house alone. One night I was awakened by a strange noise, and with some trepidation, got up to investigate. The noise was coming from the kitchen, and as I headed in that direction to investigate, I noticed an apple with bite marks on it by the fireplace on the living room floor. A lightbulb went on in my brain; I finally figured out the rats were coming down the fireplace chimney into the living room and then invading the rest of the house. I had surprised one of them mid-robbery as it was trying to take the purloined apple back up the chimney; I thought this might be an easy fix.

Next day found me on the roof examining the chimney, which was brick on the outside. The chimney had an oval masonry liner with a nice rat-sized crawl space between the external bricks and the liner. I researched how to rat-proof and found that coarse steel wool cannot be eaten by rats and forms an excellent barrier. I went straight to the hardware store and bought a lot of it. I stuffed ample quantities of the coarse material into the chimney opening. In an expanded inspection, I also found some small openings that led into the attic under an overhang, so they received the steel wool treatment, too. Rat problem solved!

Eventually we were able to get Dad stabilized, and his medical condition improved. I am sure part of his recovery was getting him out of his toxic home. In the past, he often had terrible allergic symptoms and was always hawking and hacking. The amount of cat hair (visible) and dander (invisible) in the house was probably a major contributor. He loved his cats, but did they ever shed! His VA doctor told him that he had chronic rhinitis, which means constantly inflamed/irritated sinuses and nose. To my knowledge, no one from the medical community ever visited his home to see what the indoor air quality was like. Generally, the man spent upwards of 22-hours per day inside his home breathing that dreck. No wonder he was chronically ill; his immune system was on red alert all the time.

Eventually, my dad was able to live independently again in a small apartment. Although he couldn't drive, Fresno's excellent senior transit system helped him get around town. We tried to have cleaning people help him out, but he would fire them for moving things around in his apartment. My sister did what she could to help clean, but he usually shooed her out after an hour or so.

Over the next year, Dad's mental state became more confused, but he persisted in taking care of himself as best he could. He shopped and cooked for himself until the end. Dad passed away in his own bed at home a few years ago. He was still hoarding and left my sister and Evan a nice mess to clean up at his apartment, but at least he was true to form, so there was no surprise. I was glad that he was able to do it his way.

PART VI Dave & Marla's History

Chapter 21   Dave's Early Years

When I was nine years old, my family moved from Ohio to Southern California. My mom was sick of shoveling snow from Thanksgiving to Easter. Mom was born in Akron and had experienced hard winters almost every year of her life. The catalyst for our move across the country was a winter trip to a tropical environment. My dad was a top salesman for Corning Glass, and one year his company took he and Mom to Bermuda in January. Dad attended meetings and Mom walked on the beach barefoot or swam in the warm ocean. In January! It was a revelation for her and changed our lives.

I well remember that winter, watching the Pasadena Rose Bowl parade on New Year's Day. We saw gals with bare shoulders riding in convertibles with the top down, waving at the crowd while the sun shone on the palm trees. All the while, we made do in weather well below freezing, with two feet of snow on the ground. This enticed Mom to lobby for a big change, and soon! She urged my dad to get a transfer to California or Florida, somewhere that it did not snow in winter. She did not care which place; she just did not want to go through another winter in Cleveland. Ironically, my dad was offered a very nice promotion if he would move to Corning, in upstate New York, but Mom put her foot down. After some finagling, Dad got a transfer to California in late February. We moved to Thousand Oaks, which in the early 1960s was a sleepy little town about 30 miles up the coast from Hollywood and West Los Angeles. I remember when the first stoplight was installed; now, Thousand Oaks has a population of almost 130,000 people.

As a boy, I experienced fear, suffering my share of monster-under-the-bed foolishness. I cried and made my parents come in my room to comfort me. I went through the usual angst around age 13, wondering if girls would ever like me. I finally decided to take matters into my own hands and scare myself a lot, so that eventually risk, and what could cause fear, would be just like having a fly buzzing around my ears: annoying, but not worthy of much attention. I was helped in this endeavor by several sports that are a little off the main route for high school kids, namely surfing and rock climbing.

Once my family moved from Ohio to California, I had the ocean and mountains nearby. We could get to the ocean only occasionally as it was about 20 miles away, but every time I got there, I was in the surf. The Pacific Ocean has some big waves: I have been out in 15-foot waves a few times that would probably drown a less experienced person. I taught myself to body surf around age 12, and as soon as kids in the neighborhood could drive, we scrounged up old surfboards and were off to the local surf breaks. I had many a dodgy moment being held under by a big wave that rolled me and my board right up and spit us out into what surfer's call "the soup," the foam maelstrom after a wave has broken. We learned to remain calm; we learned how to navigate back to the surface; we learned to be ready for discomfort when we ran out of air. We practiced swimming underwater laps in the high school pool to prepare ourselves for the challenges of surfing; it's possible to train the body to adapt to hypoxia, or oxygen deprivation.

Even more nerve wracking (but courage building) for me was rock climbing. There are some modest cliffs of volcanic rock near Thousand Oaks, and some pals and I scrounged up $24 for a real 150' climbing rope. We soon added carabiners, pitons, and proper climbing shoes from Europe via mail order. We were too young to drive, but a friend of my mom's, GBD, who was a proper adult – about age 30 – started driving us to Stoney Point in the eastern part of the San Fernando Valley, about 45 minutes away. We formed a small group of hard-core climbers heading out to the practice rocks every chance we could. This climbing was mainly on sandstone boulders and a few easy faces. We practiced our rope work and trained ourselves to step off a precipice and slide down the rope in rappel, sometimes free-hanging for 140 feet or so. Knowing that we would be stepping off that edge into thin air really made us check our knots! Our moms were game to have us challenge ourselves this way, but they did buy us helmets and made us promise to wear them (and a few times I was very grateful).

Pretty quickly our small group evolved into climbing trips to Tahquitz Rock in the San Jacinto Mountains near Palm Springs, where 1,000-foot faces awaited us. This climbing area had been pioneered in the mid-1930s by the Rock Climbing Section of the Sierra Club. After WWII, younger climbers such as Chuck Wilts, Royal Robbins (who founded an eponymous clothing brand), and Yvon Chouinard (who later founded Patagonia Clothing), pushed climbing to higher levels. When my pals and I appeared on the scene around 1969, a guidebook was available and many of the routes were evidenced by bolts and webbing anchors high on the faces. These Tahquitz climbs were intimidating all-day affairs requiring a high level of commitment.

We went through the usual levels of fear for beginning climbers, especially when we were hundreds of feet up a face. One common malady was known as "shaky leg" or "sewing machine leg," wherein the offending limb trembles as described. We also sweated a lot, even on cold days. The sweat was from nerves and fear. Nowadays, climbers still confront fear, but they use gymnastic chalk to keep their hands dry. Hence, in modern climbing areas, one can often identify routes by the white chalk marks showing the hand placements. We did not benefit from this. We just wiped our hands dry on our corduroy knickers and got on with the lead.

Over time, our little band started to branch out farther afield. First, we went on a few trips led by the Sierra Club Rock Climbing Section to the High Sierra faces (with GBD, the guy with a car, driving his old jeep). After we got the gist of what was required, we knocked off some of the classic climbs. Because the eastern Sierra Nevada Mountains are uplifted quite prominently, many sheer faces rise several thousand feet. One of my favorite climbs was the east face route on Mt. Whitney, which requires a seven-mile approach hike without benefit of trail. The approach starts by bashing up a gully through willow thickets, and then, above tree line, out into glaciated meadows.

I have summited twice on that route, the first time via the "Fresh Air Traverse," which requires a simple big step across a void onto a ledge that provides about 2,500 feet of direct vertical exposure to the broken rock debris below. On the second ascent, my pal Sugey Otis and I climbed a more strenuous variation that includes "Shaky Leg Crack," part of which is a daunting vertical path up an otherwise blank wall. That time, Sugey and I got to the summit just at dark, so we had to bivouac in our climbing clothes in a stone hut on the summit. It was so cold our ropes (which we were sitting on) froze to the stone floor. I have never seen a more welcome sunrise than the one the next morning.

In summer, the magnet was Yosemite Valley. Big wall routes were being pushed up almost all the main rock formations, and we stood in awe of the great climbers. In the early 1970s, climbers tended to congregate in one corner of the Valley called Camp 4. This was a free camping spot inhabited by a motley group of semi-employed climbers of varying skill and daring. I was one of the lesser skilled, but I had my share of daring companions to tackle some challenging routes. Being the first climbers of the day on a known route could be competitive, especially for the "easier" climbs, so we avoided the late-night wine drinking and campfires that some indulged in. I well remember some of the British climbers buying Budweiser in the Curry Village store and then leaving it out under a tree for the day (no cooler). We learned the Brits liked their beer warm, which was ghastly to us, but they were good climbers, so it must have worked some magic.

Usually, my crew got up before sunrise, made some tea and oatmeal, collected our climbing hardware and ropes, and caught an early national park bus to the climbing area. We would spend the day pushing up leads, swapping turns on the front. After a climb that might entail 15 rope lengths (several thousand feet), we would either rappel or hike off the side of the rock formation. We almost always got dirty--our bath was usually a swim in the Merced River when we got back to camp around dusk. One of my favorite memories was coming back from a long day, dirty and certainly aromatic, riding in a bus full of tourists. As we entered the bus near Happy Isles to go back to Camp 4, a mother grabbed several of her children and pulled them away from us. She hissed to them, "Stay away from those giant hairy climbers." We certainly had hair aplenty (it was the 70s), and covered with ropes and slings of climbing hardware, I guess we appeared giant!

In winter, the Sierra Nevada climbing areas were usually socked in with snow, so we would head to the desert. Joshua Tree is a favorite area for Yosemite climbers. When we were young, Joshua Tree was not yet a national park, so regulations were relaxed. We would often caravan from the coastal areas where we lived inland to the desert, driving in rickety VWs, old jalopies and perhaps the odd motorcycle. We prided ourselves in being "dirtbag climbers," the antithesis of the wealthy tourists in their motorhomes. We also found much humor in several tongue-in-cheek climbing publications. One of my climbing guides to the Joshua Tree area was published in 1970 by the 'Desert Rats Uninhibited.' Another early favorite was the *Vulgarian Digest,* a send-up of serious climbing magazines, published by the Lower Foothills Eating, Drinking and Farcing Society. *Descent*, another pseudo-magazine, made fun of the serious climbing publication of the American Alpine Club, *Ascent.*

The whole climbing game, much like surfing big waves, was to calculate the risk, and, if things worked out, enjoy a reward that no money can buy--the beauty of the moment. There were a few days when I did not paddle out into the lineup during the big winter swells because I knew they were out of my league. When I did go out on big days, I would catch a few waves, but mostly watch other, better surfers from my vantage point in the water. It was like that with climbing, too. Climbers love to watch each other and share the excitement of completing a hard sequence of moves or creating a bold line.

During this time period, I read works by Jack Kerouac, Henry David Thoreau, Ralph Waldo Emerson, Aldo Leopold, and John Muir. They convinced me that all that is required for solitude in the Sierra

Nevada Mountains, as with most mountain ranges, is to walk away from the road and not look back. John Muir was famous for climbing high up into a tree during a storm, like he was on the mast of a ship, to ride out the wind and feel nature's power. I was entranced by Jack Kerouac's description of time in the Sierra:

> I felt like lying down by the side of the trail and remembering it all. The woods do that to you, they always look familiar, long lost, like the face of a long-dead relative, like an old dream, like a piece of forgotten song drifting across the water, most of all like golden eternities of past childhood or past manhood and all the living and the dying and the heartbreak that went on a million years ago and the clouds as they pass overhead seem to testify (by their own lonesome familiarity) to this feeling. [3]

Leopold, Muir, and Thoreau were some of the first environmentalists who decried the destruction of nature by modern civilization, and they have been heroes and guiding lights for me ever since I discovered their works in my teens.

---

[3] Kerouac, Jack. *The Dharma Bums*. Penguin Classics, 2006.

Chapter 22   Marla's Early Years

Marla grew up in southcentral Arkansas, the youngest daughter of a Navy musician and a schoolteacher. Marla's grandparents lived nearby, and she spent lots of time with them as a young child because both of her parents worked during the day. Marla's grandparents would be considered poor today, as they did not have indoor plumbing or many modern conveniences like automatic clothes washing machines. Many of Marla's relatives hunted and grew their own vegetables; they were generally self-sufficient and lived outside the economy, only buying the few things they could not grow themselves. Some of her cousins lived near a river and subsisted almost entirely on hunting and fishing.

Marla cannot remember when she learned to read. With a teacher mother and three older sisters, she was probably reading soon after she learned to talk. At school, Marla was an excellent student, and over the course of several years, she read every book in the small school library. She also read the entire encyclopedia. This early education, coupled with her industrious nature, helped her excel at school, and she received almost straight A grades all through college and graduate school. She did receive a C in second semester physics, which still troubles her a little!

During the summers, Marla and her sister Gail worked for a local produce farm. They picked tomatoes and other food crops for 50 cents an hour. Southern Arkansas can be hot and humid, and Marla's time spent in the sun on the farm toughened her considerably. She eventually saved enough money to buy a small Honda scooter that she and her sister could ride the ten miles to their farm job. Her scooter was fun, but she was an athlete, and always loved to use muscle power when she could, so she played high school basketball and did lots of hiking and biking in the woods around their home. She also took up water skiing with her friend who had a boat, and became very adept, sometimes ripping along at 45 miles per hour. Marla saved more money to buy her first car, a red Fiat 850 convertible. She looked quite the sporty girl.

After high school, Marla moved to Texarkana, Texas to attend junior college (her family did not have the resources for a four-year institution). In these first college years, she took up with an outdoorsy lad who liked to explore caves and rock climb. She joined a group of like-minded students who spent weekends camping, canoeing, and climbing in northeast Arkansas. They did not take classes for these sports; they just rounded up some gear and headed out. Marla is unusually strong and excelled at many of these outdoor pastimes. This willingness to try new things and take calculated risks later served her well, on many levels.

After completing her first two years of college in Texarkana, Marla transferred to Texas A&M in College Station, about 200 miles south. Her first degree was in Fisheries and Wildlife Science, and she graduated Summa Cum Laude. She was subsequently accepted for a PhD program in the same field and worked as a graduate assistant for her major professors. She was only a few classes from graduating with her PhD when her major professor died, which meant she did not have a mentor for her dissertation. The project she was working on also lost funding. She took this as a bad sign and transferred into the veterinary program. She never did earn her PhD, although she was so close. All in all, Marla spent 13 years in college. Anyone who takes their cat to Marla is visiting an exceptionally well-educated doctor!

Texas has a large university system but only one veterinary school, which started about 130 years ago at A&M. It is one of the most prestigious and well-funded programs in the nation. Women were first admitted to the program on a limited basis in 1963 and then granted unrestricted admission in 1971. When Marla enrolled in the program in 1985, she was part of a class that, for the first time, had more women than men. This dramatic change was partly fueled by the popularity of a book by James Harriot entitled, *All Creatures Great and Small*. This book, by a British veterinary surgeon, told the stories of animals and their owners, and greatly popularized the profession.

For the first five years of her veterinary career, Marla worked with large animals, such as horses and cattle. She made many farm calls and drove a large pickup truck specially fitted for field medicine. Eventually, she got tired of being stepped on by 800-pound animals and decided to specialize in small animal medicine. She opened her own clinic in Waco in 1993 and has been in the same location ever since. In 2017, she was chosen by her peers as Waco's Veterinarian of the Year.

Marla believes that all work and no play make Jill a dull girl. While she worked at her Waco veterinary practice, she trained and showed Tennessee Walking Horses, and has owned as many as 15 horses at one time. Over the years, she discovered that feeding and caring for all these animals made a big dent in her bank account, so she transitioned to human-powered sports. She and a group of friends started cycling and running, and eventually took up triathlon. Marla's strongest sport is distance running, and she has completed over 100 marathons. She took up ultra-distance running in 1996, and has finished thirteen 50-mile and eleven 100-mile races. She will tell you that her crowning achievement was finishing the Western States 100 within the cutoff time.

The Western States has something of a mythical quality. It started in 1974 and is the world's oldest 100-mile race. Entry is generally by invitation (top athletes) or lottery. There are some 350 runners and 1,500 volunteers (including 100 radio operators as there is almost no cell service). The course starts near Lake Tahoe at the Squaw Valley Resort at about 6,200 feet elevation. It then crosses numerous passes, several rivers, and many steep canyons. After climbing about 18,000 feet and descending 23,000 feet, the finish is in Auburn, California (near Sacramento). Anyone finishing within 30 hours receives a bronze belt buckle and those beating 24 hours receive a silver belt buckle. Runners generally do not sleep and struggle with hydration and nutrition in later stages of the race. Temperatures can range from below freezing near pass summits to over 110 degrees in the canyons.

Marla was accepted into her first Western States in 2006. She made it about 70 miles before nausea prevented her from staying adequately hydrated and she had to stop. In 2010, she entered the lottery and won a spot for the 2011 race. While her training included running up to 70 miles per week, 100 push-ups and 200 sit-ups daily, and careful attention to diet, her real secret was to practice on the race course itself. She made numerous trips to the toughest sections of the course, which are often run in the dark during the actual race. She also practiced running extensively in snow. This paid off, as the first 16 miles of the course in 2011 was on old snow (called Sierra Cement by the locals). She also used a product containing a wasp-extract peptide called Vespa, that helps burn fat for fuel. Essentially, this allows the runner to avoid solid food. This trick prevented her from becoming nauseous, so she was able to stay hydrated, unlike her previous attempt.

During her training time in California, Marla was working overnight shifts as an emergency clinic doctor in Fresno, about three hours south of Auburn. Working overnight allowed her to take long runs during the day. On days off, she could make trips to practice on the Western States Trail itself. She was also flying back every few weeks to work at her primary clinic in Waco. As luck would have it, she was able to finish the 2011 race with three minutes to spare, and won her bronze buckle. Among all her trophies and prizes from marathons and other long races, she is proudest of her Western States buckle. She says that she will probably not go back to race Western States, as she believes in the old saying, 'One and done.' In 2016, she was national champion in her age group for 100-kilometer (at Bandera, TX) and 100-mile trail distances (at the Rocky Racoon race near Huntsville, TX).

Running 30 hours, essentially all day and all night, is often more of a mental challenge than physical. It requires the athlete to maintain constant focus because one misstep can result in a turned ankle or worse. Marla has had a few close calls. In a race in the Wasatch Mountains of Utah, Marla laid down beside a dirt road to take a wee nap at mile 70. When she woke up, she started running again and met a support vehicle. That vehicle was coming to take down an aid station. Marla was running the wrong way by herself in a mountain area she did not know. Her run for the day ended right there for safety's sake. Another time, while descending the highest mountain in Texas, Guadalupe Peak, she almost stepped on a

Mojave Green rattlesnake. The Mojave Green has the most toxic venom of any rattlesnake and without treatment, it can kill an adult. She was very lucky.

Marla's toughness and fortitude are coupled with a positive outlook and cheerfulness. These characteristics, combined with a willingness to take risks, make her the perfect partner for a fixer-upper project. And she is an amazing life partner, for which I am very grateful as well.

Epilogue

Marla's closing thoughts:
In Waco many people have known Chip and Joanna Gaines since way back. Back before there was a TV show <u>Fixer Upper</u>. Those folks knew Chip and Jo before there was Magnolia Homes renovation company or Magnolia Realty. In those days, Chip and Joanna Gaines were pretty much like any other Waco family.

I met Chip and Joanna when their star was just beginning to rise. I met Chip three times off camera. Each of those meetings with Chip deserves its own short story. Chip Gaines was at that time unguarded and relentlessly optimistic. I met Joanna Gaines once off camera. Joanna was sincere, efficient, and pragmatic. While I only met with them together as a couple in the presence of the film crew for our <u>Fixer Upper</u> episode, my lingering impression is that they had achieved balance and separation of power [or super-power] *in a way that is unique. My impression is that they are very distinct personalities who have learned to work in harmony.*

Writers' conferences often assert that everyone has a book inside them. That book would be one's autobiography. My intention with this book is not to document my life, but rather share a unique experience, that of being an accidental TV star. In truth, I *lived* in a TV star because the house is the real main character. When I was born, the Mailander House was already 44 years old. When I got my driver's license, she was 60. When Marla and I bought her and revived her, she was 104. We hope that she lives at least another 100 years and continues to inspire. At least one person has told me that she would love to have the plans for the Mailander House because she wants to build one just like it. How cool is that?

Many people recognize Marla and me on the street. While our episode was on TV originally in 2014, it has been replayed several times a month in the ensuing years. We estimate that at least 40 million people have seen the Mailander House episode. Marla was shopping one day in Austin and a young woman looked at her and said, out of the blue, "You are the veterinarian." We were in Portland, Oregon recently and the security screener looked at our identification and said jokingly, "You're from Waco. Do you know Chip and Joanna?" We said "Yes, they remodeled our house on the TV show." She did a bit of a double-take; it was cute! We said it was the house with the old bicycle on the wall. The security person knew who we were right away, even though we live 2,000 miles from Portland. However, she still made us take off our shoes and go through the scan machine. Fame only gets one so far...

Has this experience changed our lives? Yes and no. We have more financial security since we sold Mailander House to our friends Josh and Jill. We were able to take a nice trip to Italy to bicycle for two weeks last spring. I was able to fulfill a long-time dream by going up to Iowa for a trans-state bike ride called RAGBRAI. I bought a better truck (although it was used – I'm still thrifty). Marla was able to buy a vehicle (used) for a mobile veterinary practice. We still have the same friends, cut our own grass, clean our own house, and put our socks on BEFORE our shoes. We did not buy a boat or other extravagances.

We recently bought another fixer upper on short notice. One day, the house next door to Hound Haven had a big pile of children's clothes and toys dumped in the front yard. I went over and it was immediately apparent that the neighbors had moved out. The kitchen door was open and all the appliances were gone. The neighbor's dog was loose on the front porch (very unusual). She had a hurt leg and was full of fleas. Marla started feeding the dog canned food with medicines mixed in. We learned the house had been foreclosed by the bank and our neighbors evicted. Through a realtor friend, we were able to buy the house for cash with no inspections, and we closed in 10 days. We could not catch the dog, but the animal control people did and took her to the shelter to find her a new home.

Our new fixer-upper has some foundation problems caused by water getting under the house. For better or worse, I am an old hand at this now. Helped by Gail's husband, Dan, and Marla's son, Jesse, we have jacked the house up to level it. We have installed concrete and steel supports and repaired or replaced some beams and framing. Dan and I also put gutters all around to prevent further water intrusion. We hired professionals to completely rewire and install a new HVAC system. After we finish painting, we will decide whether to sell or rent it. We have applied for a zoning change so that we could legally start another vacation rental business. Whatever the outcome of this project, I am confident that our quick action to buy the house, along with strategic improvements, will prove financially smart. Just like rock climbing, one may not know the exact route up the cliff, but if they're prepared, confident, and persevere, they can succeed.

What is our end game? Next year we can retire with maximum Social Security benefits. Marla may sell her clinic. We both love to ski, and the cycling in Colorado is very good, so we might buy an old house in some little mountain town and do a bit of work on it. Know of any reality TV shows looking for some experienced actors?

Dave's Bicycle Office

Bicycle-Loving Guests at Mailander House

Guests Enjoying the Outdoor Fireplace

Marla Climbing

Dave & Friends, White Mountains

Dave & Friends, Mt. Whitney Summit

Dave & Sister Colby Rock Climbing

Dave & Marla, Bike Adventure

Skiing in the Sierra-Where it All Began!

Appendix 1: Waco History

Early History

Humans have occupied Waco for 14,000 years or more. Waco was a prime location for early Americans because two large rivers meet here. Additionally, two substantial cold-water springs provided fresh water year-round. Even in times of drought, a native village could be supplied with adequate water. Also, the fertile soil and lush grasslands provided an abundance of fish, deer, wild turkeys, wild pigs (javelina), and bison. To this the earliest residents added acorns, pecans, mesquite seeds, and many other wild plants. The native Wacoans also grew corn, squash, beans, and pumpkins. In 1824, a letter from Thomas Duke to Stephen F. Austin reported that the Wacoan native people had about 400 acres under cultivation.

At different times between 1519 and 1848, all or part of Texas was claimed by Spain, France, Mexico, The Republic of Texas, and the United States of America. A Spanish map from 1690 called Waco 'Quiscat' after the name of the chief. The Spanish reported that about 750 native people, called Wacoans because of their language, resided in permanent houses on the west bank of the Brazos River, spread between the two fresh water springs.

In the late 1820s, some Cherokee groups being driven west from their homes in the eastern US started to move into the Waco region. These Cherokees apparently wanted dominance over the region and within months drove the Wacoans westward. The original Wacoan people were eventually relocated north to reservations in Indian Territory, in what is now Oklahoma.

The first permanent Anglo settlement in the area was a trading post established in 1844 by a Connecticut Yankee named George Bernard. The principal trading items brought to barter at the store were hides, dressed and undressed, of deer, bison, bear, raccoon, fox, beaver, bobcat, and panther. Deerskin was the most common, and each skin earned between 12 and 17 cents in trade. A few years later, Scotsman Neil McLennan moved into the area near the mouth of the Bosque. McLennan County, of which Waco is the county seat, is named after him.

By the 1850s, since the Cherokee and Comanche had stopped attacking settlers, Europeans moved into the area, and George Erath and Jacob de Cordova surveyed for a new townsite. Lands were purchased for as little as $1/acre from Spanish land grant holders. On May 5, 1849, Erath's suggestion for the town name of "Waco Village" was agreed upon.

The Civil War and Reconstruction

Before the Civil War, cotton was the prime crop, and in 1859 the county's population was 749 free people and 1,938 slaves. The Texas constitution made slavery overtly legal and prohibited an owner from freeing slaves without specific legislative approval. As northern opposition to slavery increased and local talk of leaving the union grew, Sam Houston visited Waco in 1860 and delivered an address appealing against succession. But after Republican Abraham Lincoln was elected, the state of Texas followed southern neighbors into the Confederate States of America.

An estimated 2,200 white men left McLennan County to fight for the Confederacy, and Waco contributed five men who became Confederate generals and other officers. During the war, vast herds of longhorn cattle were neglected and became half-wild. Therefore, starting about 1866, enterprising cattlemen gathered up the free-ranging animals and drove them to markets in Kansas and Nebraska. The famous Chisholm Trail passed through Waco so that longhorns could ford the Brazos. Tens of thousands of cattle, often driven by some rough characters, passed through Waco after the Civil War. To commemorate this period, brass statues of three cowboys, representing an Indian, a freed slave, and a Mexican, along with about 20 longhorn cattle have recently been placed near the crossing at Indian Springs Park.

In 1868, a group of prominent citizens decided that a bridge across the Brazos was needed and raised $130,000 to build it using a new suspension technology. After it was finished, the Waco Suspension Bridge was the longest single-span bridge in the world, and it charged a toll for everyone crossing for the next 20 years. In 1871, Brooklyn, NY followed Waco by building its own suspension bridge of a similar design. Today only bicycles and pedestrians use the Waco Suspension Bridge, but it is an icon of the community.

Post-Civil War, many free blacks settled in their own communities and had their own churches, cemeteries, schools, and shops. McLennan County had its share of Ku Klux Klan rallies and terrorist activities, among them lynchings. Because of widespread violence across the South, the Klan was suppressed by the federal government, and most groups disbanded. In the early 1900s, oil and gas were found about 50 miles east of Waco. Much of the profit found its way to Waco banks and investors. Many of the classic old homes of Waco, such as the Migel House on Washington and 15th streets, were built with oil money.

In 1861, the Waco Classical School became Waco University. In 1886, the Baylor University name and possessions were moved from Independence, Texas, and became Baylor University at Waco. Texas Christian University moved to Waco in 1895 from Thorpe Springs, and Paul Quinn College, the oldest black college in Texas, moved to a campus on Elm Avenue in Waco in 1881. Thus, for several decades in the late 19th century, Waco was the educational center of the entire state, referred to as, "The Athens of Texas."

In contrast to the higher education institutions, during this post-war period many saloons and gambling establishments also sprang up, most also offering "ladies of the night." Waco for a time had the nickname of "Six Shooter Depot" due to the many armed drifters and westward travelers. In July 1878, the notorious robber Sam Bass and his men stopped for a drink at Waco's Ranch Saloon, and Bass paid for whiskey with a $20 gold piece called a 'double eagle.' That double eagle was the last of the 3,000 which remained from a major train robbery near Big Springs, TX. After his Waco drinking session, Bass and his gang headed south to Round Rock, where a trap set by the Texas Rangers sealed their fate.

In 1893, William Cowper Brann, a gifted writer, started a monthly publication called *Brann's Iconoclast*. Within a few years, he had made many friends and enemies and he started carrying a Colt 45 revolver (the gun that won the West) everywhere he went in public. After a particularly strong (written) attack by the *Iconoclast* upon Baylor University in 1898, a supporter of Baylor, Tom E. Davis, fired a shot from a Colt 45 into Brann's back as he passed by. Brann spun around and emptied his six-shooter toward Davis, four rounds finding their mark. Davis was carried into a nearby office while Brann was taken to the police station. Only when officers noticed that Brann's shoes were filled with blood did they realize the fatal nature of his wound. Brann died that night and Davis the next day. One can see a marker for this famous shootout on the west side of Fourth St. between Austin and Franklin avenues. (Brann's home, now gone, was on 5th St., just across from the Mailander House.)

World War I Era

The Ku Klux Klan had a resurgence around WW I, and violence against blacks and minorities broke out in many areas. For example, "When Waco Klan No. 33 tried to march in the small Central Texas town of Lorena, [about 12 miles from Waco] the sheriff of McLennan County tried to stop the demonstration, touching off a riot in which several people were wounded, and one man stabbed to death." [4]

In 1916 a terrible public lynching occurred when convicted murderer Jesse Washington was grabbed after the trial by an angry mob on the courthouse steps. He was tortured, mutilated, and burned alive over two hours before being killed, all witnessed by about 15,000 residents. Local law enforcement officials did not try to stop the carnage. National newspaper photographers (in town for another reason) recorded the atrocity. Pictures of the repugnant

---

[4] "Ku Klux Klan," Texas State Historical Association. https://tshaonline.org/handbook/online/articles/vek02

lynching were published in newspapers across the nation, giving Waco a huge black eye that lasted for decades.

The NAACP used this lynching in its campaign to force law enforcement agencies to act, which worked to some degree. For instance, in 1923, Waco Sheriff Leslie Stegall protected a convicted black man, Roy Mitchell, from mob lynching. Interestingly, some of the history books written by local authors, such as former Waco Mayor Roger Conger, do not mention these incidents at all.

As the United States entered WW I, Waco officials lobbied for and received a large training base called Camp MacArthur. Over 80,000 Army recruits, mostly from Michigan and Wisconsin, were trained here. The Army successfully petitioned for the brothels on 2nd St. to be closed to prevent venereal disease from spreading among the troops (condoms were not legalized in the United States until a decade later). Much of the area that was Fort MacArthur is now housing, schools, and recreational areas, such as the Heart O' Texas Fairgrounds and Lions Park.

World War II Era

Waco is very proud of one of her local sons, Doris Miller. Miller, a black man, grew up on a farm outside Waco. He was a good student and fullback on his high school football team. As a boy he hunted rabbits and birds to help feed his family. In 1939, he joined the US Navy and became a Mess Attendant Third Class, one of the few Navy positions open to blacks at the time. He received some gunnery training in 1940, probably as an ammunition carrier, and was transferred to the battleship West Virginia in August, 1941 at Pearl Harbor, Hawaii.

On Sunday, December 7, 1941, he arose at 06:00 and helped serve officer's mess at 07:00. Just before 08:00 during a surprise attack, the first of ten Japanese torpedoes hit the West Virginia, and 'battle stations' was sounded. Miller reported to his assigned anti-aircraft station, but the gun had been destroyed in the initial attack. An officer then ordered Miller to accompany him to the bridge to help move wounded Captain Bennion to a sheltered spot behind the conning tower. During this time, a fire started on deck and on the surrounding ocean fed by leaking fuel.

During the fire and continued attacks by aircraft strafing, bombs, and torpedoes, Miller loaded ammunition into anti-aircraft guns aft of the conning tower. While not familiar with the 50-caliber machine gun, he manned the starboard gun while another white seaman fired from the port gun. Some accounts suggest that Miller shot down a handful of Japanese planes, but in the chaos of battle it was hard to confirm. Miller fired the gun until ammunition was exhausted and then helped move the captain out of thick oily smoke from the many fires onboard. During the continuing attack, several Japanese armor-piercing bombs penetrated the deck, and five more torpedoes found their mark on the West Virginia. As the heavily damaged battleship was sinking, Miller and other seamen moved wounded sailors through oil and water to the quarterdeck for evacuation.

After Pearl Harbor, several white members of the House and Senate submitted bills to award Miller the highest battle decoration, the Medal of Honor. Navy Secretary Knox vetoed this idea, as blacks had never been given this award. Instead, the Commander in Chief of the Pacific Fleet, Admiral Nimitz, pinned the Navy Cross on Miller, which at the time was the third highest award for gallantry in combat. The citation reads:

> For distinguished devotion to duty, extraordinary courage, and disregard for his own personal safety during the attack on the Fleet in Pearl Harbor, Territory of Hawaii, by Japanese forces on December 7, 1941. While at his captain's side on the bridge, Miller, despite enemy strafing and bombing and in the face of a serious fire, assisted in moving his Captain, who had been mortally wounded, to a place of greater safety, and later manned and operated a machine gun directed at enemy Japanese attacking aircraft until ordered to leave the bridge. [5]

---

[5] "Cook Third Class Doris Miller's Navy Cross Citation," Naval History and Heritage Command,

Miller became a hero to the black press, which was agitating to allow black service members to serve in all capacities (rather than just mess hall workers or cooks). He was sent on a recruiting/speaking campaign stateside to help sell war bonds. In May 1943, he reported for sea duty on the escort carrier USS Liscome Bay. In the eastern Pacific, during the Battle of Makin, before dawn on November 24, 1943, the Liscome Bay was struck in the stern by a torpedo, and a few minutes later, the bomb magazine detonated. The ship sank in twenty-three minutes, and Miller's body was never found. In addition to the Navy Cross, Miller was entitled to the Purple Heart Medal; the American Defense Service Medal, Fleet Clasp; the Asiatic-Pacific Campaign Medal; and the World War II Victory Medal. Commissioned on 30 June 1973, USS *Miller* (FF-1091), a Knox-class frigate, was named in honor of Doris Miller. The City of Waco and private donors have raised about $2.5 million for a permanent Doris Miller memorial, which was dedicated December 7, 2018 near the suspension bridge.

The Branch Davidians

Waco is known as the location of a tragic stand-off involving a religious sect (the Branch Davidians). This sect split off from the Seventh Day Adventists in the early 1930s and built a compound in a rural area called Mount Carmel, about 10 miles southeast of Waco proper. Over time, several charismatic men and women led the group until it was taken over by Vernon Howell in the early 1980s. Howell eventually changed his name to David Koresh and saw himself as the Lamb of God who would usher in the Messiah.

For a time, the Davidians were quiet and accepted in the community. David Koresh had a rock band that played on Friday nights at a local bowling alley. He and his followers shopped at the local grocery stores. They were weird but did not bother anyone, so the local sheriff mostly left them alone. In 1993, due to allegations

---

The African American Experience in the U.S. Navy, Doris Miller's Navy Cross Citation. https://www.history.navy.mil/content/history/nhhc/browse-by-topic/diversity/african-americans/miller/doris-millers-navy-cross-citation.html

of polygamy and arms dealing, the Branch Davidian compound was raided by dozens of armed agents from the Bureau of Alcohol, Tobacco, and Firearms. The Davidians were heavily armed themselves and fought back tenaciously. Four federal agents were killed and sixteen wounded. Five Davidians were killed early in the assault and a sixth was shot five times in the back by federal agents as he tried to enter the compound, returning from work in town.

Because federal agents were killed, the FBI took over the operation and a 51-day siege began. The national press descended upon the area, and Waco was the nearest town with an airport, hotels, and restaurants. Hence, the town of Waco became inextricably connected to the news reporting of the siege 10 miles away. The FBI were able to have 19 children released, albeit without their parents. Eventually, the FBI brought in military equipment from nearby Fort Hood and staged a day-long attempt to break into the compound using heavy machine guns and tear gas. Eventually the large wood building housing the Davidians caught fire and 76 people died, among them many children. Subsequently, 12 survivors were indicted on various charges and about half went to prison, although all have been released now.

A monument for the officers killed at Mt. Carmel, along with other law enforcement officers, sits on the western Brazos riverbank near the Suspension Bridge. Monuments to the 76 Davidians who died during the siege are at Mt. Carmel. Several television specials have been made about the cult and siege, and almost a dozen books have been written on the topic. Although it occurred over 25 years ago, the tragedy is still in many people's memory.

Appendix 2: Mailander Family History

Fred and/or Charles Mailander were the builder/s of the Mailander house, the subject of this book. Charles Mailander was born in Germany in 1847 and immigrated to the US in 1879 or 80 (records vary). His children, Fred (age five) Rudolph (age four), and a daughter (age one) also emigrated at this time. After moving to the US, Charles married a German woman about eight years his junior named Minnie, or Mina, in 1884.

The Mailander's first home was at Ninth and Clay streets, about three blocks from what is now the Magnolia Market at the Silos. Charles Mailander was a carpenter, contractor, builder, and manufacturer of office and bank fixtures, with a shop at 614 Webster St (right across the street from the current Magnolia Market). His son, Frederick Mailander, was also a carpenter.

Charles resided at Mailander House, built in 1910, with his wife until his death in 1918 at age 71. His wife, Minnie Louise Mailander, lived in the house until her death in 1933, and is buried with her husband at Oakwood Cemetery. Gertrude Wilhelmina Nake Henjes, born in Germany, was a Mailander on her mother's side. She resided in the house from about 1933 until her death of a heart attack in 1961. After she died, the house was purchased by a neighbor and rented to college students. (In fact, one of our guests lived at this house in the 1980s when she was at Baylor, and she said her cat loved to sleep on the window shelf in the front room).

Construction of The Waco German Evangelical Zion's church was supported by Charles Mailander, who loaned the congregation about 25% of the cost of construction, which they repaid at no interest within seven years. Located at 629 S. Eighth St., the frame church was built by the Mailanders in 1882. It later burned and was rebuilt in brick for $10,000.

Just prior to World War II, Fred Mailander assisted Otto and Hilde Levy, Jews in danger from the Nazis, in relocating to the U.S. after they had experienced multiple unsuccessful attempts to emigrate. In addition to securing their visas, Mr. Mailander provided the Levys with a house and covered the cost of moving their furniture. As Hilde said, "And when we arrived here in Waco was Mr. Mailander, and he kissed us, 'Welcome to America.'"

An interview conducted by the Baylor Institute for Oral History with Grace Hasseltine Jenkins Garrett Kee in 1980 reveals some additional insights into Fred Mailander. For example, "Mr. Mailander was a lover of flowers, especially roses; and all on the walks and the curbs he had rose trees . . . he wore a red rose or red carnation every day of the world. If he didn't have something in his own yard, he came down—he always walked to work from out on Austin—and he'd stop in at Wolfe the Florist and get one for his coat—never without it."[6]

According to Kee, Mailander ". . . could have weathered the Depression, but he would not change his line of furniture, and at that time the stores were wanting more modern furniture and didn't want mahogany."[7] Mailander made some attempt to produce updated furniture (and keep his workers employed), but ultimately the business closed as the demand for quality furniture declined and Mailander refused to lower his craftsmanship standards.

---

[6] Oral Memoirs of Grace Hasseltine Jenkins Garrett Kee (1980). Waco and McLennan County Project, Baylor University Institute for Oral History, 1986. digitalcollections.baylor.edu/cdm/ref/collection/buioh/id/1241
[7] Ibid

Appendix 3: Bicycle History

The first bicycles, called penny-farthings, had different size wheels (a giant one in front) that made them difficult to ride and the crashes spectacular. Those first bikes had direct drive – there was no chain. They were called "wheels" specifically because that is what the rider sat upon. Interestingly, the first roads were paved at the insistence of cyclists.

In the late 1880s, the "safety bicycle" was developed with two equal sized wheels and a chain drive from the pedals to the rear wheel. These bicycles were relatively easy to make, and tens of millions of bicycles were in use in America before WW I. They were cheap to build and purchase, easy to ride, and durable.

Women in the United States bought bicycles by the hundreds of thousands since the bicycle allowed them to work outside the home. Thirty years before American women were given the right to vote, suffragettes promoted women's cycling as a form of liberation from men's financial control. Clothing changed too – bloomers were a response to women cycling. Bloomers morphed into trousers, and slowly but surely women's clothing gained equal utility to men's.

The following quotes from women cyclists capture how liberating the bicycle was for them:

"Let me tell you what I think of bicycling. I think it has done more to emancipate women than anything else in the world. It gives women a feeling of freedom and self-reliance. I stand and rejoice every time I see a woman ride by on a wheel … the picture of free untrammeled womanhood." Susan B. Anthony [8]

"Don't be afraid of people's expectations of you. Don't be afraid of going fast and getting hurt. You can always wear black stockings to cover up the scars! You just have to forget what your parents taught you – stuff like being careful, looking good, and catching the best man available." Marla Streb, World Single Speed Champion [9]

---

[8] Strickland, Bill. *The Quotable Cyclist*, 2nd ed. Halcottsville, NY: Breakaway Books, 2001.
[9] Ibid

"The bicycle was the first machine to redefine successfully the notion of what is feminine. The bicycle came to symbolize something very precious to women - their independence." Sally Fox [10]

"I've seen women who've gotten into mountain biking who really come alive after just a few months. They're radiant, they've lost weight, their shoulders are back, and they're no longer taking any crap from their husbands." Carol Waters [11]

Many people love vintage bikes. Unfortunately for us, during WWII metal drives, untold thousands (perhaps millions) of bikes were gathered up from barns and sheds and melted down for the war. Steel was also needed to expand the oil industry as petroleum became the life blood of the war effort. During this time, the US economy changed fundamentally, and the bicycle lost its position as primary transportation thereafter.

The Velvet Road Racer that Joanna found us was built just five years before our house. In 1905, there were probably thousands of shops across America building bicycles. By the late 1880s, any competent blacksmith could order materials and create his own bike frames. Therefore, our Velvet Road Racer could have been built almost anywhere in the USA.

---
[10] Ibid
[11] Ibid

References

Kerouac, Jack. *The Dharma Bums*. Penguin Classics, 2006.

Oral Memoirs of Grace Hasseltine Jenkins Garrett Kee (1980). Waco and McLennan County Project, Baylor University Institute for Oral History, 1986. digitalcollections.baylor.edu/cdm/ref/collection/buioh/id/1241

Smithwick, Noah. *The Evolution of a State, or Recollections of Old Texas Days*. Austin: Steck Company, 1935.

Strickland, Bill. *The Quotable Cyclist*, 2nd ed. Halcottsville, NY: Breakaway Books, 2001.

Tzu, Chuang. "When the Shoe Fits" from *In the Dark Before Dawn: New Selected Poems of Thomas Merton*. New Directions, 2005.

About the Author

Dave Morrow never thought he would move to Waco, Texas. But good fortune brought him together with his life partner, Marla Hendricks, a successful veterinarian who has practiced in Waco for almost 25 years. A free spirit, Dave has traveled by bicycle and on foot in many countries and has visited all 50 US states. At age 18, he walked the Pacific Crest Trail, which, in 1973, was more an idea on a map than a completed route on the ground (he got lost a lot). Later, he spent 10 weeks trekking and climbing in the Himalayas, several months bike touring in New Zealand and Europe, and drove an old car on a 10,000 km adventure into the outback of Australia. He has climbed mountains all over the western US, New Zealand, Nepal, and Morocco.

In Waco, his challenge was caring for a beautiful 108-year-old home built by German craftsmen and remodeled by Magnolia Homes. He and Marla currently own three older homes in Waco, the youngest of which is 66 years old. He believes that homes can age gracefully (like fine wine) with good care. He is currently restoring, with his brother-in- law, a cottage home built in 1930.

Dave has authored many scientific and technical papers, and taught in the Civil and Environmental Engineering Department at California Polytechnic State University, San Luis Obispo. Dave currently has a beautiful Pinarello track bike in his office to inspire his work. He and Marla still reside in Waco with Thumpy, a 14-year-old Treeing Walker Coonhound (named for the sound of his tail on the floor).

www.ingramcontent.com/pod-product-compliance
Lightning Source LLC
Chambersburg PA
CBHW020417080526
44584CB00014B/1370